አዲስ እትም

New edition

በማስተማር ሂደት ውስጥ የተባበሩትን ድርጅቶች ከልብ አመሰግናለሁ እነሱም

መድኃኒዓለም የኢትዮጵያ ኦርቶዶክስ ተዋህዶ ቤተ ክርስቲያን
Ethiopian Orthodox Tewahedo Our Savior Church at Riverside NY.NY

ቅድስት ሥላሴ የኢትዮጵያ ኦርቶዶክስ ተዋህዶ ቤተ ክርስቲያን
Holy Trinity Ethiopian Orthodox Tewahedo church Bronx, NY

ጽዮን ቅድስት ማርያም የኢትዮጵያ ኦርቶዶክስ ተዋህዶ ቤተ ክርስቲያን
St. Mary of Zion Ethiopian Orthodox Tewahedo church Yonkers, NY

አዋቂ የአማርኛ ትምህርት ተሳታፊዎች
(My Adult Amharic class participant NY, NY)

I appreciate all churches, all colleges and students that have been in my class over the years. I have learned from all of you. I thank you all.

ምስጋና

ዶ/ር ርብቃ ማሞ
ዶ/ር ያሬድ ተካበ
ዶ/ር ፍቅሬ ቶሎሳ
አቶ ዮናስ አሰፋ
አድባር የኢትዮጵያ ሴቶች አንድነት ማህበር ቦስተን

ልጆች እንዳስተምር ትልቅ ትብብር ያደረጉ
የትምህርትና ድርጅት ሃላፊዎች

ዶ/ር ጉዌን ሊ ሳይክ
ዶ/ር አንጀላ ሃይክ
አቶ ኩዌክ ይ

ያለፈቃድ አሳትሞ ገበያ ላይ ማዋል በህግ ያስጠይቃል!

Many thanks

The following people for their assistance, supporting the idea and in editing the very first edition of this book:

Rebecca Mammo MD. Mph
Yared Tekabe Ph.D.
Mr. Yonas Assefa
Fikere Tolosa, Ph.D.
Adbar Ethiopian Women's Alliance (Boston)

I appreciate

I appreciate these people for providing space and allowing me to introduce the Amharic language to children and adults of the Berkeley, Piedmont and Oakland area of California.

Gwen Rowe-lee Sykes Ph.D.
Angela Haik Ph.D.
Mr. Kwock Yee

E-mail: Lakech_One@yahoo.com

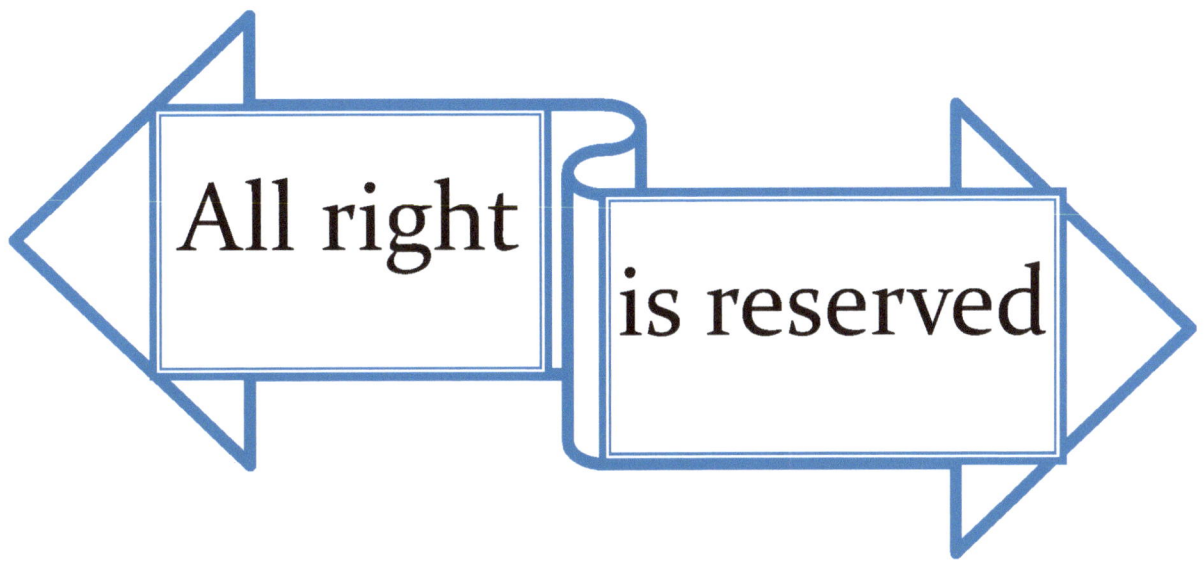

No part of this book may be reproduced in any form without written permission from the publishers, except by the reviewer who may quote brief passages in a review to be printed in a newspaper or magazine

10% of the sales of Laqech-one will be donated to ESAC (Ethiopian Social Assistance committee)

ማሳሰቢያ

ይህ የአማርኛ መማሪያ መጽሐፍ የተዘጋጀው በውጪ ሃገር ላሉኢትዮጵያውያን ቤተሶችና እንዲሁም ቋንቋውን ለማነገር ለሚፈልጉ ሁሉ ነው ። በተለይ ጥንታዊ የሆነው የኢትዮጵያ ታሪክ ና ስልጣኔ ለማወቅ በየአድባራቱ ተከማችተው ያሉትን ጥንታዊ መጻሕፍትን ለመራመር ለሚሹ ሁሉ ጥሩ መነሻ ነው።

በመሆኑም የመጀመሪያ (Laqech-One) እትም በሥራ ላይ በዋለበት ጊዜ በተገኘው ልምድና አስተያየት ታርሞ ቋንቋውን በማዳበር ተዘጋጅቶ የቀረበ መጽሐፍ ነው።

ከዚህ ጋር ተከታይ ላቀች ሁለትና ሶሥት መጽሐፍ ይገኛል፤
Laqech-Two and Laqech-Three also available:

ተግባራቱም

ላቀች አንድ (Laqech- One)
ፊደል፣ ቃላትን፣ አነባብን አጻጻፍን ያስተዋውቃል
Introduces Fidel, writing, words and reading

ላቀች ሁለት (Laqech-Two)
ቃላትንና ጽሑፍን ያጠናክራል ያስተምራል
Teaches writing and vocabulary

ላቀች ሦሥት (Laqech-Three)
ጽሑፍና ንባብን ያጠናክራል ያስተምራል
Teaches writing and reading

ሰው ያለውን ካካፈለ ንፉግ አይባልም ከታሪክ ወቀሳ ለመዳን የተደረገ ጥረት ነውና በዚህ ሂደት አብረን እንጓዋዝ ።

አዘጋጂና ጸሐፊ
ዘውዲቱ ፍስሐ

መግቢያ

ላቀች አንድ Laqech-one ከተወልደበት እ አ አቆጣጠር ታህሳስ (December 2000) ጀምሮ ብዙ ኮፒ ተዘጋጅቶ ለአስተያየት ተበትኖ በተገኘው የገንቢ ሃሳብ በመመርኮዝ እንዲሁም ላለፉት ተከታታይ ዓመታት አማርኛ በማስተማር በተገኘው ልምድ ና አስተያየት ጋር በማገናዘብ ለሁለተኛ ጊዜ ታርሞና ተጨማሪ ዝርዝር በመያዝ በተጠናከረ ሁኔታ የቀረበ ነው።

(Laqech-one) የመንደርደሪያ ቃላት አማርኛ መማሪያ መጽሐፍ ዋና ዓላማ ቋንቋ የባሀል መሰረት እንደ መሆኑ ሁሉ ከባህላቸው ና ከቋንቋቸው ለተራራቁ እንዲሁም ከኢትዮጵያ ውጪ ለተወለዱ ኢትዮጵያውያን ወጣቶች፣ በጋብቻ፣ በሥራ፣ በማደጎ ፣ በተለያየ ምክንያት አማርኛ ለማወቅ፣ ምርምር ለፈለጉ ሁሉ እንዲያገለግል የተዘጋጀ ነው ።

ላቀች አንድ(Laqech-One) የአማርኛ መማሪያ መጽሐፍ የሚጀምረው ቀን በቀን የምንጠቀምበትን ነገሮችን በመያዝ መሰረታዊ የአማርኛ አነጋገር ዘይቤ በማካተት ቋንቋውን ለመማር እንዲያመች ፈደልን በማስለየት ፣ ቃላትን በሥዕል፣ ቃላትን ከእንግሊዘኛ አናባቢ ጋር ከነ ትርጉሙ፣ በማስደግፍ የቤት ቁሳቁስ፣ የዱር አራዊት፣ የቤት እንስሳትን፣ በከተማ በገጠር፣ የሰውነት ክፍሎች፣ የምግብ ዓይነቶችን ፣ መሰረታዊ አማርኛ ቁጥሮችን በመያዝ ለጀማሪ ተማሪዎች በቀላል ዘዴ በማለማመድ አማርኛ ቋንቋን ለማርና ለማወቅ እንዲረዳ የተዘጋጀ መጽሐፍ ነው።

ከዚህ በላይ ለማወቅ ከፈለጉ በታላላቅ ኢትዮጵያዊ ሊቃውንቶች የተጸፈውን አማርኛ መማሪያ መጽሐፍትን ኢትዮጵያ ውስጥ ስለሚገኝ ያንን በመጠቀም ዕውቀትን ማዳበር ይቻላል

ይወቁት

ይህ መጽሐፍ የተዘጋጀው ካለ አስተማሪ እራስን በራስ ለመርዳት እንዲሁም ቂንቄ ለማንበብና ለመናገር እንዲያስችል በመሆኑ ዕውቀትን ለመለካት መለማመጃውን በመሥራት በዚህ መጽሐፍ መጨረሻ ገጽ ላይ በማመሳከር ደረጃን መለካት ያስችላል።

Note: The book is prepared for self teaching to help you figure out your knowledge and after figuring out through the excerices you may refer back to collaborate page of the book.

ተጨማሪ

ይህ የመንደርደሪያ ቃላት አማርኛ መጤያ መጽሐፍ አማርኛም ሆነ እንግሊዘኛ ለመማር ለሚፈልጉ ሁሉ ጠቃሚ መሳሪያ ነው።

Learning Amharic for English speakers or Amharic speakers, Laqech One Amharic script book is a useful tool for both languages.

Introduction

In this activity book you will find most of the Amharic key words which will help you learn and read Amharic, the official language of Ethiopia. It is designed for reading and speaking this language. Many of the exercises are inspired by the kind of games used to teach children to read their own languages: matching game, memory games, joining exercises, and so on.

For those who are interested in learning the language, it is a friendly introduction to reading and writing Amharic. There is a section to review all your new words and the Answers to all the activities to check yourself.

This Laqech-One book is a flexible fun way of reading your first words in Amharic. It should give you a head start whether you're learning at home privately or in a group.

Script Part

The purpose of this part of the text is to introduce you to the Amharic script and how it is formed. You should not try to memorize the alphabet or to write the letters yourself. Instead, study the words in each topic, look back at the Amharic letters and understand the meaning of the words. Remember, though, that recognizing the whole shape of the word in an unfamiliar script is just as important as knowing how it is made up. Using these methods you will have a much more instinctive recall of vocabulary and will gain the confidence to expand your knowledge.

The Amharic Script is not nearly as difficult as it might seem at first glance. The Amharic alphabets originally came from Ge-eze a language, which the Ethiopian Orthodox Church has been using for centuries up to the present day.

The Alphabet and Syllables

There are 231 letters in the Amharic alphabet. It is better to try to know and recognize them all immediately, but more importantly to try understand the principles of how the alphabet works and then use the charts as you work through the book.

Unlike English, Amharic words are generally spelled as they sound, although there are some exceptions to this rule. There is no capital or lower case letters. The letters making up each syllable are written together to form a sound or meaning.

A syllable consists of alphabets:

1	ሀ	ha	ሁ	hu
2	ለ	le	ሉ	lu
3	መ	me	ሙ	mu
4	ሰ	se	ሱ	su
5	ሸ	she	ሹ	shu

Pronunciation and Reading

Some time an alphabet can repeat them to create words.

        1   እማማ/emama
        2   አባባ/ ababa
        3   አበባ/ abeba
        4   ቱቱ/ tutu
        5   ኩኩ/ kuku
        6   ዲዳ / dida

Here the letters

1 ma-ma
2 ba-ba
3 Ku-ku
4 di-da   creates a word.

Exactly how each combination of letters is written in a syllable side, within each other, etc. is determined by the shape of the letters? A feeling for this will develop as you become more familiar with the script.

Furthermore some Amharic letters have unique alphabets which (phonetically) sound the same but distinct from each other in script. Of the 231 alphabets there are 194 letters used in daily spoken language where as they remain letters used in advanced Amharic literature.

Those alphabets are:

ሃ-ሐ-ሓ	ሠ	ኅ-ኃ	ፀ	ዓ-አ
ha	se	ha	tse	aa

There is no exact English sound for the following alphabets.

ቀ	ኽ	ጠ	ጨ	ጸ	ጰ
qe	heh	teh	cheh	tse	peh

One must practice with an instructor to learn the unique way these sounds are pronounced

* We use about 194 alphabets
* Letters making up syllables are written together in order

Making Words

Some Amharic words are made up of three or more syllables:

        1 ላም/lam-cow
        2 በር/berr-door (open)
        3 ጋራ/gara-hill
        4 ጀርባ/jerba-back
        5 ባቡር/babur-train
        6 አንበሳ/anbesa-lion
        7 ጣት/taht-finger
        8 ጎጆ/gojo/small house-shack
        9 መዘጊያ/mezegiya-door (closed)
        10 መውጫ/mewecha-exit

Pronunciation and Reading

To understand the Amharic alphabet, the exercises have simplified some aspects of the pronunciation in order to emphasize the basics.

Some Amharic sounds are similar to their English equivalents, but others need special attention. The same letters can also be pronounced in a slightly different way depending on their position in a syllable, and this is reflected in the pronunciation given for the individual words.

Here are some to note

1. ሻይ- shay/tea
2. ዕቃ- ehqa/thing or Goods
3. ና- na/comes here (m)
4. ክንድ-kened/arm
5. ያ-ya/over there or that
6. ጸሎት-tselot/prayer

Things to remember:

*   Amharic words are pronounced with more emphasis.

*   Many Amharic sounds are not familiar to the English speaker.

*   There is no capital letters in Amharic Words.

ፊደል/Fidel

ተራ/row	1	2	3	4	5	6	7
ሀ/1	ሀ	ሁ	ሂ	ሃ	ሄ	ህ	ሆ
	ha	hu	hi	haa	hey	h	ho
ለ/2	ለ	ሉ	ሊ	ላ	ሌ	ል	ሎ
	le	lu	li	la	ley	l	lo
ሐ/3	ሐ	ሑ	ሒ	ሓ	ሔ	ሕ	ሖ
	ha	hu	hi	haa	hey	h	ho
መ/4	መ	ሙ	ሚ	ማ	ሜ	ም	ሞ
	meh	mu	mi	ma	mey	m	mo
ሠ/5	ሠ	ሡ	ሢ	ሣ	ሤ	ሥ	ሦ
	se	su	si	sa	sey	s	so
ረ/6	ረ	ሩ	ሪ	ራ	ሬ	ር	ሮ
	re	ru	ri	ra	rey	r	ro
ሰ/7	ሰ	ሱ	ሲ	ሳ	ሴ	ስ	ሶ
	se	su	si	sa	sey	s	so
ሸ/8	ሸ	ሹ	ሺ	ሻ	ሼ	ሽ	ሾ
	she	shu	shi	sha	shey	sh	sho
ቀ/9	ቀ	ቁ	ቂ	ቃ	ቄ	ቅ	ቆ
	qe	qu	qi	qa	qey	q	qo
በ/10	በ	ቡ	ቢ	ባ	ቤ	ብ	ቦ
	be	bu	bi	ba	bey	b	bo
ተ/11	ተ	ቱ	ቲ	ታ	ቴ	ት	ቶ
	te	tu	ti	ta	tey	t	to

ፊደል/Fidel

ተራ/row	1	2	3	4	5	6	7
ቸ/12	ቸ	ቹ	ቺ	ቻ	ቼ	ች	ቾ
	che	chu	chi	cha	chey	ch	cho
ሀ/13	ሀ	ሁ	ሂ	ሃ	ሄ	ህ	ሆ
	ha	hu	hi	haa	hey	h	ho
ነ/14	ነ	ኑ	ኒ	ና	ኔ	ን	ኖ
	ne	nu	ni	na	ney	n	no
ኘ/15	ኘ	ኙ	ኚ	ኛ	ኜ	ኝ	ኞ
	gne	gnu	gni	gna	gney	gn	gno
አ/16	አ	ኡ	ኢ	ኣ	ኤ	እ	ኦ
	aa	au	ai	aa	aey	a	ao
ከ/17	ከ	ኩ	ኪ	ካ	ኬ	ክ	ኮ
	ke	ku	ki	ka	key	k	ko
ኸ/18	ኸ	ኹ	ኺ	ኻ	ኼ	ኽ	ኾ
	heh	huh	hih	hah	heyh	heeh	hoh
ወ/19	ወ	ዉ	ዊ	ዋ	ዌ	ው	ዎ
	whe	wu	wi	wa	wey	w	wo
ዐ/20	ዐ	ዑ	ዒ	ዓ	ዔ	ዕ	ዖ
	aa	au	ai	aaa	aey	a	ao
ዘ/21	ዘ	ዙ	ዚ	ዛ	ዜ	ዝ	ዞ
	ze	zu	zi	za	zey	z	zo
ዠ/22	ዠ	ዡ	ዢ	ዣ	ዤ	ዥ	ዦ
	zje	zju	zji	zja	zjey	zj	zjo

ፊደል/fidel

ተራ/row	1	2	3	4	5	6	7
ጀ ፐ /23	የ	ዩ	ዪ	ያ	ዬ	ይ	ዮ
	ye	yu	yi	ya	yey	y	yo
ጀ ዐ /24	ደ	ዱ	ዲ	ዳ	ዴ	ድ	ዶ
	de	du	di	da	dey	d	do
ጀ ፈ /25	ጀ	ጁ	ጂ	ጃ	ጄ	ጅ	ጆ
	je	ju	ji	ja	jey	j	jo
ጀ ጌ /26	ገ	ጉ	ጊ	ጋ	ጌ	ግ	ጎ
	ge	gu	gi	ga	gey	geh	go
ጀ ጊ /27	ጠ	ጡ	ጢ	ጣ	ጤ	ጥ	ጦ
	teh	tuh	tih	tah	tey	teeh	toh
ጀ ጡ /28	ጨ	ጩ	ጪ	ጫ	ጬ	ጭ	ጮ
	cheh	chuh	chih	chah	chehy	cheeh	choh
ጀ ፀ /29	ጰ	ጱ	ጲ	ጳ	ጴ	ጵ	ጶ
	peh	puh	pih	pah	pehy	peeh	poh
ሗ /30	ጸ	ጹ	ጺ	ጻ	ጼ	ጽ	ጾ
	tse	tsu	tsi	tsa	tsey	tseh	tso
ሗ ፅ /31	ፀ	ፁ	ፂ	ፃ	ፄ	ፅ	ፆ
	tse	tsu	tsi	tsa	tsey	tseh	tso
ሗ ፈ /32	ፈ	ፉ	ፊ	ፋ	ፌ	ፍ	ፎ
	fe	fu	fi	fa	fey	f	fo
ሗ ፐ /33	ፐ	ፑ	ፒ	ፓ	ፔ	ፕ	ፖ
	pe	pu	pi	pa	pey	peh	po

Note to Instructors

The New Laqech-One is a unique language learning tool for students of *Amharic and English*. It provides students with compendium of useful vocabulary to converse in Amharic.

The Laqech-one book is designed to provide the learner of Amharic with systematic and enjoyable word practice.

The Beginner's workbook is divided into ten week for one hour lesson or five weeks for two hour lessons.

Each lesson in the Laqech-one book focuses on specific subject matter. The format is such, however, that instructors may choose to fit any class schedule.

Instructors will note that the varied exercises throughout the Laqech-one book are structured to help the student acquire beginning basic learning skills needed, and as a building block for further study.

Laqech two and Laqech three books follow to complete your learning, speaking, writing and reading of Amharic. I hope and believe that these books help you better understand the Ethiopian language, culture, and history.

ማውጫ/mawcha
Table of contents

ክፍል ፩ Part one

1-1............... በከተማ/beketema.............in city
1-2............... በገጠር/begetter...............country side
1-3............... እንሰሳት/enesesat..............Animals

*ቁጥር /quter....................numbers

ክፍል ፪ Part two

2-1.......የቤት ቁሳቁስ/yebet qusaquse..... Home items
2-2.................ልብስ/lebes................... clothes
2-3.................ምግብ/megeb................. food

*ተፈላጊ ቃላት/tefelagi qalat.... useful words

ክፍል ፫ Part three

3-1...................ሰውነት/sewenete..............human body
3-2............... ቀናት/qenat...................days
3-3............... ቀለማት/qelemat...............colors

*ማመሳከሪያ/mamesakeriya.........................corroborate

ክፍል ፩

Part One

ክፍል አንድ Part one
Around city-በከተማ
Look at the pictures of things you might see around City

1. ምግብ ቤት/megeb bet- Restaurant

መሶብ /Mesob-Dining basket

Cont.....around City

2. ሱቅ/suq-shop

3. መንገድ/meneged-road

Cont... around the City

4. ትምህርት ቤት/Temhret bet-School

5. ታክሲ/taxi-taxi

Cont... around the City

6, ባቡር/babure-train

7. ሆቴል/hotel-hotel

Cont… around the City

8. አውቶቡስ/autobus-bus

9. መኪና/mekina-car

Cont… around the City

10. ትልቅ ቤት/teleq bet- big house

11. ሲኒማ ቤት/ cinema bet - Movie Theater (house)

Cont… around the City

12. ብስክሌት/beskelet- bicycle

13. መጠጥ ቤት/metet bet-bar

Match the Amharic script to the Amharic pronunciations.

1.	ቤት	1.	autobuse/bus
2.	አውቶቡስ	2.	megeb bet/restaurant
3.	ባቡር	3.	bet/house
4.	ምግብ ቤት	4.	babure/train
5.	ብስክሌት	5.	besklet/bicycle
6.	ሱቅ	6.	taxi/taxi
7.	ታክሲ	7.	suq/shop
8.	ሲኒማ ቤት	8.	hotel/hotel
9.	መንገድ	9.	temhert bet/school
10.	ትምህርት ቤት	10.	meneged/road
11.	መኪና	11.	cinima bet/movie house
12.	ሆቴል	12.	mekina/car
13.	ጋቢና	13.	mekina maqomia/parking
14.	ጎማ	14.	gabina (driver's seat)
15.	መኪና ማቆሚያ	15.	goma /tire

Match the Amharic script to the Amharic pronunciations.

1. posta bet/post office	1. መጠጥ ቤት
2. ሱቅ	2. ፖስታ ቤት
3. metet bet/bar	3. suq/shop
4. meneged/road	4. mekina/car
5. መኪና	5. ቤት
6. bet/house	6. መንገድ
7. cinima bet /movie house	7. ቡና ቤት
8. ሻይ ቤት	8. ሲኒማ ቤት
9. buna bet/coffee house	9. shaybet/teahouse(room)
10 ዳቦ ቤት	10. መታጠቢያ ቤት
11. metatebiya bet/bath room	11. ፍርድ ቤት
12. fredbet/court	12. dabo bet/bakery

Choose the Amharic word that matches the picture.

1.

መልስ/mels-answer____

1-1. ቤት/bet   1-2. ሲኒማ ቤት/Cinema bet   1-3. መንገድ/meneged

2.

መለስ/mels-answer____

2-1. መንገድ/eneged   2-2. ሱቅ/suq   2-3. ባቡር/babur

Cont….. match the picture.

3.

መልስ/mels-answer____

3-1. ሲኒማ ቤት/cinima bet 3-2. መንገድ/meneged 3-3. ባቡር/babur

4.

መልስ/mels-answer____

4-1. ሱቅ/suq 4-2. ትምህርት ቤት/Temhert bet 4-3. ትልቅ ቤት/teleq bet

Cont….matches the picture.

5.

መልስ/mels-answer____

5-1. መኪና/mekina   5-2. ባቡር/Babur   5-3. አውቶቡስ/autobus

xxxxxxxxxxxxxxxxxxxxxxxxxxxxxxxxxxxxxxxxxxxxxxxxxxxxxxxxxxxxxxxxxx

6.

መልስ/mels-answer___

6-1. ትምህርት ቤት/temhert bet   6-2. ሲኒማ ቤት/cinema bet   6-3. ቤት/bet

Look at the signs and their meanings.

1. ትምህርት ቤት አካባቢ/temhert bet akababi-school zone

2. አውቶቡስ መጠበቂያ/autobus metehbeqiya-bus stop

3. የባቡር መስመር/yebabur mesmer-trainline/track

Cont..... their meanings.

4. ሆቴል/Hotel-hotel

5. የመኪና መንገድ/yemekina meneged-car road

Match each number to the correct picture.

1. ትምህርት ቤት አካባቢ /temhert bet akababiy
2. አውቶቡስ ማቆሚያ /autobus maqomiya
3. ሆቴል/hotel
4. ባቡር መስመር / train line
5 መኪና መንገድ/mekina meneged
6 ምግብ ቤት/ megeb bet

a   bus stop   b. school zone   c.   hotel

  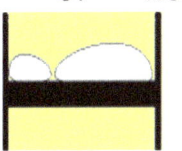

___   ___   ___

d, restaurant   e, car road   f. train

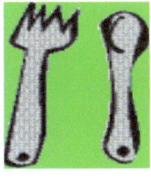  

___   ___   ___

Look at the picture of things you might see around City.

1. ምግብ ቤት/megb bet-restaurant

መሶብ/mesob-dining basket

Cont..... might see around City.

2. ሱቅ/suq/shop

ሽቀጣ ሽቅጥ/sheqe sheqet - commodity

3 የግር መንገድ/ye eger meneged- walking road

Cont..... might see around City.

4. ትምህርት ቤት/temhert bet

5. ባቡር/babure

Cont..... might see around City.

6. መኪና/mekina-car

7.የመንገድ መብራት/yemenged mebrat-street light

Match each Word to correct Picture.

1. ምግብ ቤት/megb bet   a

2. ቤት/ bet   b

3. ሲኒማ ቤት/cinima bet   c

4. አውቶቡስ/autobus   d

5. ሱቅ/suq   e

Choose the Amharic Word that matches the picture.

1. -------

a. መንገድ/menged   b. ትምህርት ቤት/temhert bet   c. ሱቅ/suq

xxxxxxxxxxxxxxxxxxxxxxxxxxxxxxxxxxxxxxxxxxxxxxxxxxxxxxxxxxxxxxxxxxxxxxxxxxx

2. ---------

a. ትምህርት ቤት/temhert bet   b. ባቡር/babur   c. መንገድ/menged

xxxxxxxxxxxxxxxxxxxxxxxxxxxxxxxxxxxxxxxxxxxxxxxxxxxxxxxxxxxxxxxxxxxxxxxxxxx

3. _____

a. ትምህርት ቤት temhert bet   b. መንገድ/meneged   c. ሲኒማ ቤት/cinima bet

Cont…..matches the picture.

4._____

a ሲኒማ ቢት/cinima bet   b. ቤት /bet   c. ትምህርት ቤት/temhert bet

5._____

a ሲኒማ ቢት/cinima bet   b. ቤት /bet   c. ትምህርት ቤት/temhert bet

ድብልቅ ቃል መማር
Learn Mixed Words

Look at the Amharic words and their English meanings and how to pronounce them.

1. ሃይማኖት
   haymanot
   Religion

2. ቄስ
   qes
   Priest

3. ገበታ
   gebeta
   dining table

4. የጠረጴዛ ልብስ
   ye terpeza lebes
   table cloth

5. መጽሐፍ ቅዱስ
   metshaf qedus
   Holy book/Bible

6. መጽሐፍ
   mesthaf
   book

7. መጽሔት
   metshet
   magazine

8. ጋዜጣ
   gazeta
   newspaper

9. መደርደሪያ
   mederdriya
   shelf

10. ሳጥን
    saten
    wooden box

11. ማስመሪያ
    masmeriya
    ruler

12. መሰላል
    meselal
    ladder

ድብልቅ ቃል መማር
Learn Mixed Words

Look to the Amharic words to English meaning and their pronunciation

1. ሼክ/sheke
   teacher/leader
   (in muslim religion)

2. ኢማም/emam(asegaj)
   prayer leader
   (in muslim religion)

3. መስጊድ/ mesgid
   worship Place

4. አጋንንት/aganent
   evil spirit

5. ገሃነም/ gehanem
   hell

6. ገነት/genet
   paradise

7. ገበያ/gebeya
   market

8. መናፈሻ/menafesha
   park

9. አቅጣጫ/aqetacha
   direction

10. ምስራቅ/meseraq
    east

11. ምእራብ/merab
    west

12. ሰሜን/semen
    north

13. ደቡብ/debub
    south

14. ቀኝ/qegn
    right

15. ግራ/gera
    left

16. ወደፊት/wodefit
    forward

17. ወኋላ/wedhula
    backward

18. ቀጥታ /qeteta
    straight

19. ቁልቁል/qulqul
    downward

20. አቀበት/aqebet
    upward

Match the mixed Amharic Words to English meanings.

1. ሃይማኖት/haimanot
2. ሼክ/shek
3. መስጊድ/mesgid
4. ኢማም/emam
5. ቄስ/qes
6. መጽሐፍ ቅዱስ/mestehaf qedus
7. ጋዜጣ/gazeta
8. መጽሔት/metshet
9. መጽሐፍ/metsehaf
10. መደርደሪያ/mederderiya
11. ማስመሪያ/masemeriya
12. የጠረጴዛ ልብስ/yeterpeza lebes
13. ወደኋላ/wedhula
14. አቀበት/aqebet/
15. ቀጥታ/qeteta
16. ወደፊት/wodefit
17. ግራ/gera
18. አቅጣቻ/aqetacha
19. ቀኝ/qegn
20. መናፈሻ/menafesha

1. priest
2. prayer place
3. muslim teacher
4. religion
5. head of prayer place
6. newspaper
7. Bible/holy book
8. Book
9. magazin
10. tablecloth
11. shelf
12. ruler
13. upward
14. forward
15. backward
16. straight
17. park
18. right
19. left
20. direction

Match the Amharic words to English words

1. አውራ ጎዳና/aewra godana
2. ጎጆ ቤት/gojo bet
3. ትልቅ ቤት/telq bet
4. ተማሪ/temari
5. ምግብ/megeb
6. ገበያ/gebeya
7. ሸቀጥ /sheqeteh
8. የጭነት መኪና/yechenet mekina
9. ህዝብ ትራንስፖርት/hzeb transport
10. አዳራሽ/adarash
11. አጥር/atehr
12. የትራፊክ መብራት/ye trafic mebrat
13. የግር መንገድ/ye eger menged
14. መስቀለኛ መንገድ/mesqelnga menged
15. ዳቦ ቤት/dabo bet
16. የመንገድ ዳር ሱቅ/yemenged dar suq

1. shack/hut
2. high way
3. food
4. big house
5. market
6. student
7. truck
8. a hall
9. commodity
10. traffic light
11. public transportation
12. fence
13. street shop
14. bakery
15. Sidewalk
16. cross road

በገጠር/be Geter(Country Side)

Look at the pictures of things you might find in countryside.

1. ተራራ/terara=mountain

2. ኮረብታ/korebeta=hill

Cont…..in countryside.

3. ድልድይ/deldey=bridge

4. ሜዳ/meda=field

በገጠር/be Geter (Country Side)

Cont… countryside.

5. ወንዝ/wenz=river (Hudson River New York)

6. ሃይቅ/hayq=lake

Cont….in countryside.

7. አበባ/abeba=flower

8. ፀሐይ/tsehay=sun

Cont….in countryside.

9. ጫካ/chaka=forest

10. ምድረበዳ/mdrebeda=desert

Cont….in countryside.
11. ዛፍ/zaf=tree

12. አርሻ/ersha=farm

Find out how much you know by joining the Amharic words with their English meaning and pronunciation as in the example below:

ምሳሌ/mesale- ex. ሃይቅ/hayq---------lake

1. ተራራ	1. meda/field
2. ሜዳ	2. terara/mountain
3. አበባ	3. bahr/sea
4. ባህር	4. abeba/flower
5. ወንዝ	5. ersha/farm
6. ምድረበዳ	6. wenz/river
7. አርሻ	7. mdrebeda/desert
8. ፀሐይ	8. korpeta/hill
9. ኮረፓታ	9. deldy/bridge
10. ድልድይ	10. tsehay/sun

Match all the words to the pictures

1. ምድረ በዳ/mdrebeda   a-desert

2. ሃይቅ/hayq   b-lake

3. እርሻ/ersha   c-farm

4. አበባ/abeba   d-mountain

5. ባህር/bahr   e-flower

6. ተራራ/terara   f-sea

Match all the words to the pictures

7. ወንዝ/wenz

g - hill

8. ኮረፕታ/korepeta

h - river

9. ዛፍ/zaf

I - forest

10. ሜዳ/meda

J - tree

11. ጫካ/chaka

k - bridge

12. ድልድይ/deldy

L - field

Look at the pictures and their meanings.

1.ከብቶች/kebtoch= farm animals

2. ደን/den=forest

Cont...their meanings.

3. መንደር/mender-small village

4. ዳገት/daget=hill

Cont…their meanings.

5. ቀበሮ/qebero-fox

6. ንብ/neb

Cont…their meanings.

7. ጋራ /gara- Mountain

8. እንሰት/enset - false banana tree

Note: Enset is a main food in south, and south west of Ethiopia. It is also known by the name of qocho. Enset produces. Qocho is favored by the Ethiopians as a delicacy.

Cont...their meanings.

9. ሽንኮራ አገዳ shenkora ageda-sugar cane

10. መቃ/meqa-bamboo

Check the features in the Landscape and see how many word you can find.

1. ፀሐይ/tsehay-sun
2. ጫካ/chaka-forest
3. ተራራ/terara-mountain
4. ሜዳ/meda-field
5. ድልድይ/deldy-bridge
6. አበባ/abeba-flower
7. ወንዝ/ wenz-river
8. ዛፍ/zaf-tree
9. እርሻ/ ersha-farm
10. መንገድ/menged-road
11. ኮረብታ/korebeta-hill
12. ከብቶች/kebtoch-farm animals

ገጽ/page 41

Match and connect the Amharic Word to its Pronunciation

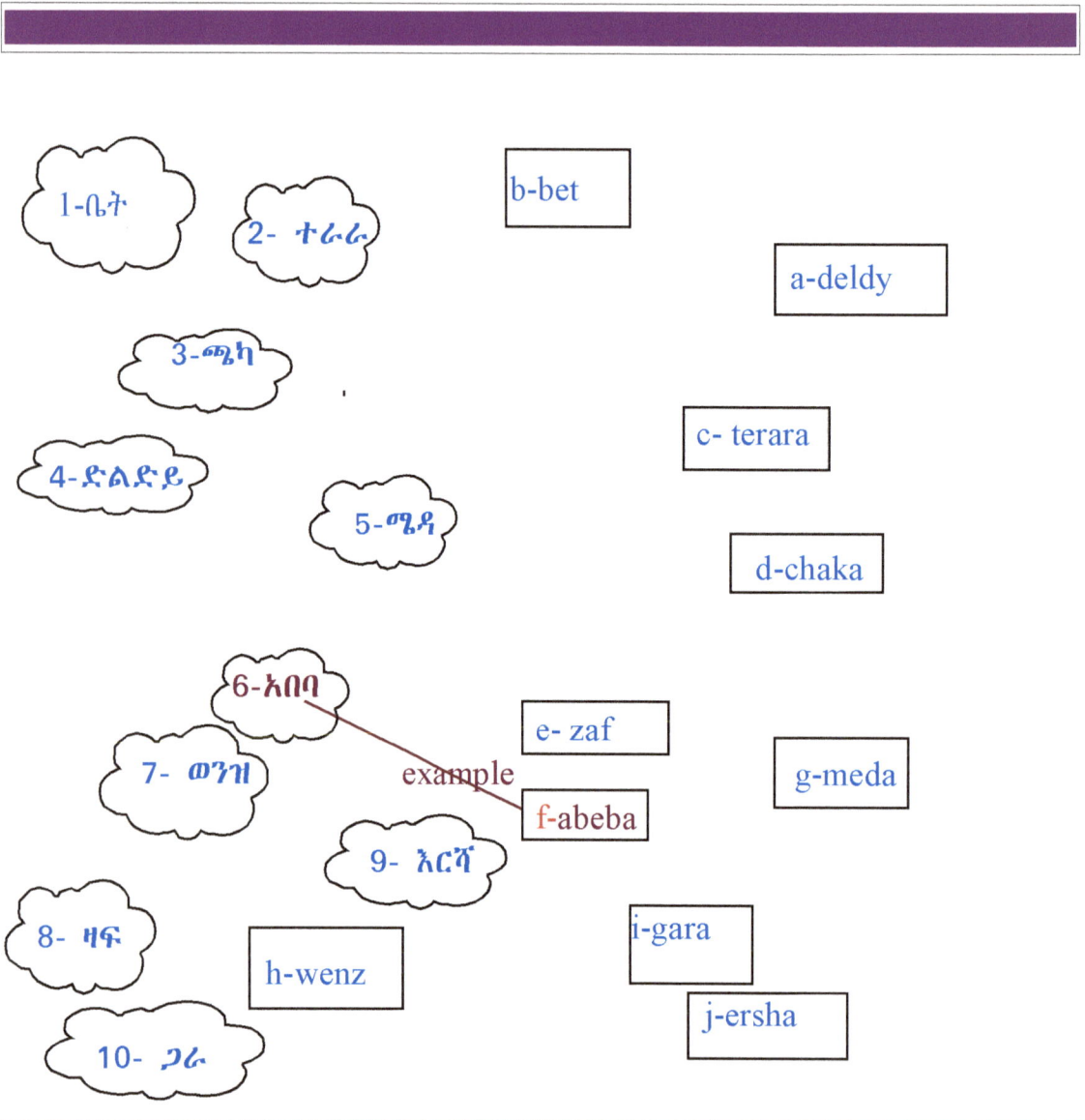

Match the Amharic Words and their Pronunciation

1	ዛፍ	1-	tsehay
2	ጫካ	2.	ersha
3	ድልድይ	3.	bet
4	ወንዝ	4.	kebtoch
5	እርሻ	5.	zaf
6	አበባ	6.	deldy
7	ፀሐይ	7.	chaka
8	ቤት	8.	terara
9	ከብቶች	9.	wenz
10	የርሻ መኪና	10.	abeba
11	ሜዳ	11.	yersha mekina
12	ተራራ	12.	meda
13	ንብ	13.	qebro
14	መንደር	14.	den
15	ቀብሮ	15.	nb
16	ደን	16	mender

Find these Amharic Words in the word square.

The words can run left to right or top to bottom

1. ጫካ
2. ዛፍ
3. ወንዝ
4. ድልድይ
5. አበባ
6. ቤት
7. ሜዳ
8. ንብ
9. ቀብሮ
10. መንደር

	1	2	3	4	5	6	7	8
1	ዉ	ወ	ን	ዝ	አ	በ	ባ	ጫ
2	ድ	ል	ድ	ይ	በ	ዛ	ፍ	ካ
3	ጨ	ካ	ሜ	ዳ	ን	ቀ	መ	አ
4	ዛ	ቤ	ት	ን	ብ	በ	ን	ጬ
5	ፍ	ቀ	በ	ሮ	መ	ሮ	ደ	ለ
6	ወ	ዛ	ላ	ጠ	ጣ	ሄ	ር	ማ
7	ድ	ራ	ሜ	ዳ	ፉ	ደ	ፍ	ር
8	ር	ቤ	ት	መ	ን	ደ	ር	ቃ

Learn new words

Look at the pictures and their meanings and pronunciation

1.ውሃ/weha-water

2.ብርጭቆ/berchiqo-glass

Cont...... meanings and pronunciation.

3   ሲኒ/sini-cup

4. ሹካ/shuka- fork

Cont…… meanings and pronunciation.

5. **ማንኪያ**/mankiya-spoon

6. **ሳህን**/sahen-plate

Cont...... meanings and pronunciation.

6. **ጀበና**/jebena-kettle

ሲኒ/sini/cup

*note: Jebena (the picture you see) is the Ethiopian version of coffee pot but every coffee pot or tea pot is called Jebena.

7. **ማማሰያ**/amamaseya-spatula

Cont…… meanings and pronunciation.

9. መጥበሻና ድስት/metehbesha na dst-frying pan and pot

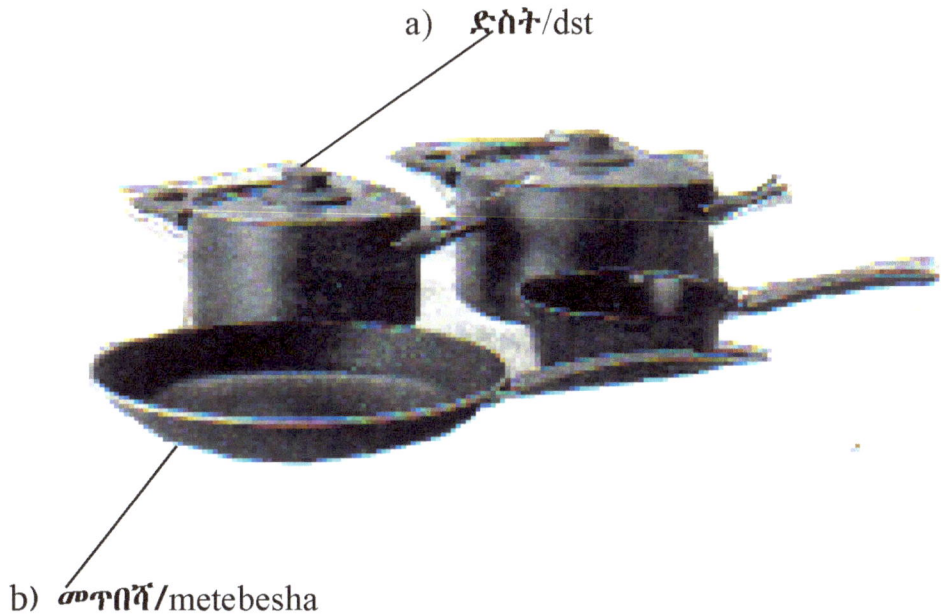

a) ድስት/dst

b) መጥበሻ/metebesha

10. ቅጠል/qetel-leaf

Cont...... meanings and pronunciation.

11. ጀልባ/jelba-boat

11, ወቂያኖስ/weqiyanos-ocean

Note: Pacific Ocean under the Bridge (Golden get bridge San Francisco

Cont…… meanings and pronunciation.

2. ባሕር ዳር/bahrdar-sea shore

13. መርከብ/merkeb-ship

Cont...... meanings and pronunciation.

14. ጃንጥላ/jantla-umbrella

15. ከረባት/kerebat-tie

Cont…… meanings and pronunciation.

16. መስታወት/mestawt-mirror

17. ሚዶ./mido-comb

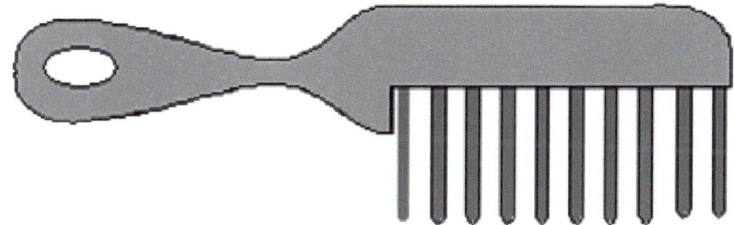

Cont…… meanings and pronunciation.

18. ሻሽ/shash-scarf

19. ወጥ ቤት/wetbet-kitchen

Cont...... meanings and pronunciation.

20. ቢላዎ/bilawo-knife

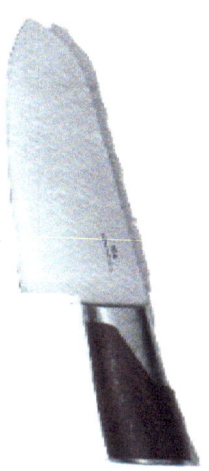

21. መክተፊያ/mektefiya-cutting board

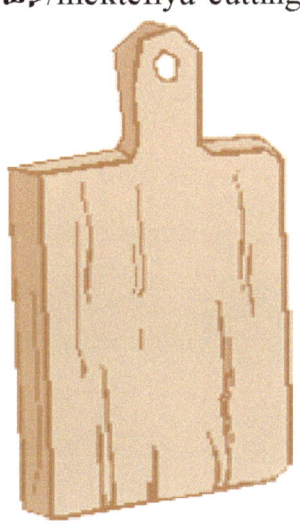

Cont...... meanings and pronunciation.

22 ቁልፍ/qulef- button

23. ቁልፍ/qulf- key

ቃላት/qalat-words

1. ከባድ/kebad-heavy
2. ቀላል/qelal-light
3. ርካሽ/rekash-cheap
4. ውድ/wed-expensive
5. ንፁህ/netsuh-clean
6. ቆሻሻ/qoshasha-dirty
7. ትልቅ/teleq-big
8. ትንሽ/tenesh-small
9. ፈጣን/fetan-fast
10. ቀርፋፋ/qerfafa-slow
11. አዲስ/adis-new
12. አሮጌ/arogey-old

Match the Amharic words to the meaning and pronunciation

1. ወጥ ቤት　　　　　　　　1. bilawo-knife

2. ፈጣን　　　　　　　　　2. jantela-umbrella

3. ብርጭቆ　　　　　　　　3. fetan-go fast

4. ቢላዎ　　　　　　　　　4. weha-water

5. ውሃ　　　　　　　　　　5. berchiqo-glass

6. አሮጌ　　　　　　　　　6. qoshasha-dirty

7 ቁልፍ　　　　　　　　　7. arogey-old

8 አዲስ　　　　　　　　　8. wetbet-kitchen

9. ቆሻሻ　　　　　　　　　9. qulf-button

10 ሻሽ　　　　　　　　　　10. adis-new

11, መክተፊያ　　　　　　　11. kerebat-tie

12. ሚዶ　　　　　　　　　12. shash-scarf

13. ከረባት　　　　　　　　13. mido-comb

14. ጃንጥላ　　　　　　　　14. mestawt-mirro

15. መስታወት　　　　　　　15. mektefiya-cutting board

Join the Amharic words to English comparable.

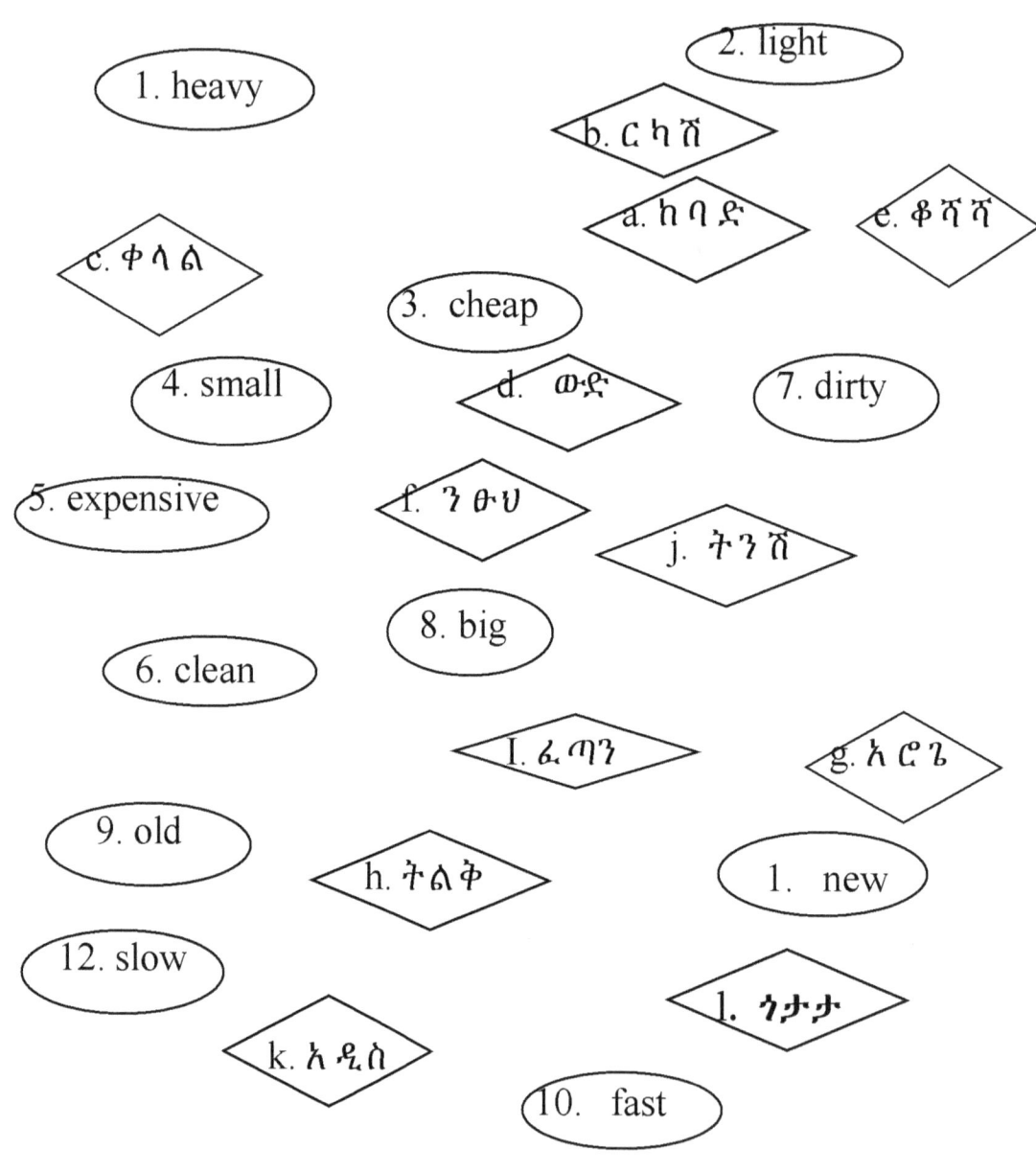

ገጽ/page 58

እንስሳት/ensesat-Animals

Cont.....pronunciations and their meanings.

1. **አንበሳ**/anbesa-lion

2. ውሻ/wesha-dog

እንስሳት/ensesat-Animals

Cont.....pronunciations and their meanings.

3. በግ/beg-lamb

1 ላም/lam-cow

ገጽ/page 60

እንስሳት/ensesat-Animals

Cont.....pronunciations and their meanings.

5. ፈረስ/feres-horse

6. ዝንጀሮ/zenjero-monkey

እንስሳት/ensesat-Animals

Cont.....pronunciations and their meanings.

7.አህያ/aheya-donkey

8.ጥንቸል/tenchel-rabbit

እንስሳት/ensesat-Animals

Cont.....pronunciations and their meanings.

9.አይጥayet-mouse

10. .ሰጎን/ segon-ostrich

እንስሳት/ensesat-Animals

Cont.....pronunciations and their meanings.

10. **ቀጭኔ/** qechny-giraffe

11. **ነብር/**neber-tiger

እንስሳት/ensesat-Animals

Cont.....pronunciations and their meanings.

12. ዝሆን/zehon-elephant

13. የሜዳ አህያ/ymeda aheya-zebra

እንሰሳት/ensesat-Animals

Cont.....pronunciations and their meanings.

14.ጉጉት/gugut-owl

15.ጨሉሌ/chuleley-hawk

እንስሳት/ensesat-Animals

Cont.....pronunciations and their meanings.

17.እርግብ/ergeb-pigeon

18. **ግንደ ቆርቁር**/gendqorqur-woodpecker

እንስሳት/ensesat-Animals
Cont.....pronunciations and their meanings.

19. ጋጋኖ/gagano-pelican

20. ዓሳ/asa-fish

እንሰሳት/ensesat-Animals

Cont.....pronunciations and their meanings.

21. ዳክዬ/daky-duck

22. ወፎች/ wofoch-birds

እንሰሳት/ensesat-Animals
Cont.....pronunciations and their meanings.

23. ድመት dmet-cat

24. ግመል gmel-camel

እንስሳት/ensesat-Animals

Cont…..pronunciations and their meanings.

25. እባብ/ebab – snake

26. ምንጭ/mnech-stream

Find how much you know by joining the Amharic words to English meaning and their pronunciation.

1.	ቀጭኔ	1.	chuliley-hawk
2.	ሰጎን	2.	qechiney-giraffe
3.	ድመት	3.	segon-ostrich
4.	ጩልሌ	4.	dmet-cat
5.	በሬ	5.	gendqorqur-woodpecker
6.	ግንደ ቆርቁር	6.	bery-bull
7.	ነብር	7.	doro-chicken
8.	ምንጭ	8.	nebr-tiger
9.	ጉጉት	9.	lam-cow
10.	ዶሮ	10.	ergeb-pigeon
11.	ፈረስ	11.	ebab - snake
12.	ዳክዬ	12.	gugut-owl
13.	ላም	13.	mnch-stream
14.	እርግብ	14.	feres-horse
15.	እባብ	15.	daky-duck

Find the Amharic words listed below in the cross-word puzzle.

The words can run left to right or top to bottom

1. ዓሳ/asa
2. ድመት/dmet
3. እርግብ/ergb
4. ውሻ/wesha
5. እባብ/ebab
6. በግ/beg
7. ዝንጀሮ/znjero
8. ዝሆን/zehon
9. ወፎች/wefoch
10. ግመል/gmel

CROSS WORD PUZZLE/semterez-ሰንጠርዝ

	1	2	3	4	5	6	7	8	9
1	በ	ድ	እ	ዉ	ት	ዝ	ዝ	ወ	ቀ
2	ግ	መ	ር	ግ	ዝ	ን	ጀ	ሮ	ወ
3	እ	ት	ገ	ዝ	ሆ	ን	ዓ	ሣ	ፎ
4	ባ	ግ	መ	ል	ን	ዉ	ወ	ፎ	ች
5	ብ	ብ	ድ	ብ	በ	ግ	ዉ	ሻ	ድ
6	ዉ	ዓ	መ	ስ	እ	ር	ግ	ብ	መ
7	ሻ	ሳ	ት	እ	ባ	ብ	መ	ጣ	ት

ገጽ/page 73

Pets and Animals

	አማርኛ Amharic	pronunciation	meaning
1	ድመት	dmt	cat
2	ውሻ	wsha	dog
3	ዶሮ	doro	chicken
4	ፈረስ	feres	horse
5	አህያ	ahya	donkey
6	በሬ	bery	bull
7	ላም	lam	cow
8	ፍየል	feyel	goat
9	በግ	beg	sheep
10	አሳማ	asama	pig
11	ዝንጀሮ	znjero	monkey
12	በቅሎ	beqlo	mule
13	ጥንቸል	tnchel	rabbit
14	ተርኪ	turky	turkey
15	ኤሊ	aeli	tortoise

Find how much you know by joining the Amharic words to English meaning and their pronunciation.

1.	ዓሣ	1.	beg-lamb
2.	በግ	2.	ebab- snake
3.	እባብ	3.	eregb-pigeon
4.	ጋጋኖ	4.	asa-fish
5.	እርግብ	5.	gagano-pelican
6.	ግመል	6.	znjero-monky
7.	ዳክዬ	7.	wefoch-birds
8.	ዝንጀሮ	8.	gmel-camel
9.	ወፎች	9.	dakey-duck
10.	ዝሆን	10.	zehon-elephant
11.	ጉጉት	11.	fyel-goat
12.	ፍየል	12.	gugut-owl

ገጽ/page 75

Find out which Amharic word does not fit the group.

as in the example * ሰ ው/sew-እ ር ሻ /ersha-ሜዳ /meda

ተራ	ሀ	ለ	ሐ
1	ሀ/በር-ber	ለ/በሬ-berey	ሐ/ላም-lam
2	ሀ/ፍየል-fyel	ለ/ነብር-neber	ሐ/በግ-beg
3	ሀ/ድመት-dmet	ለ/ዶሮ-doro	ሐ/ዳክዬ-daky
4	ሀ/አህያ-ahya	ለ/ፈረስ-fres	ሐ/አንበሳ-anbesa
5	ሀ/አሳማ-asama	ለ/ጥንቸል-tnechel	ሐ/አይጥ-ayet
6	ሀ/ሴት-set	ለ/ወንድ-wend	ሐ/ድብ-deb
7	ሀ/ሙዝ-muz	ለ/ወይን-weyn	ሐ/ዝሆን-zhon
8	ሀ/ቀሚስ-qemis	ለ/ሱሪ-sori	ሐ/መንገድ-menged
9	ሀ/መኪና-mekina	ለ/አውቶቡስ-atobus	ሐ/ሎሚ-lomi
10	ሀ/እርሳስ-eresas	ለ/ብዕር-bear	ሐ/ሳህን-sahen

Find and connect the Amharic word to the English word.

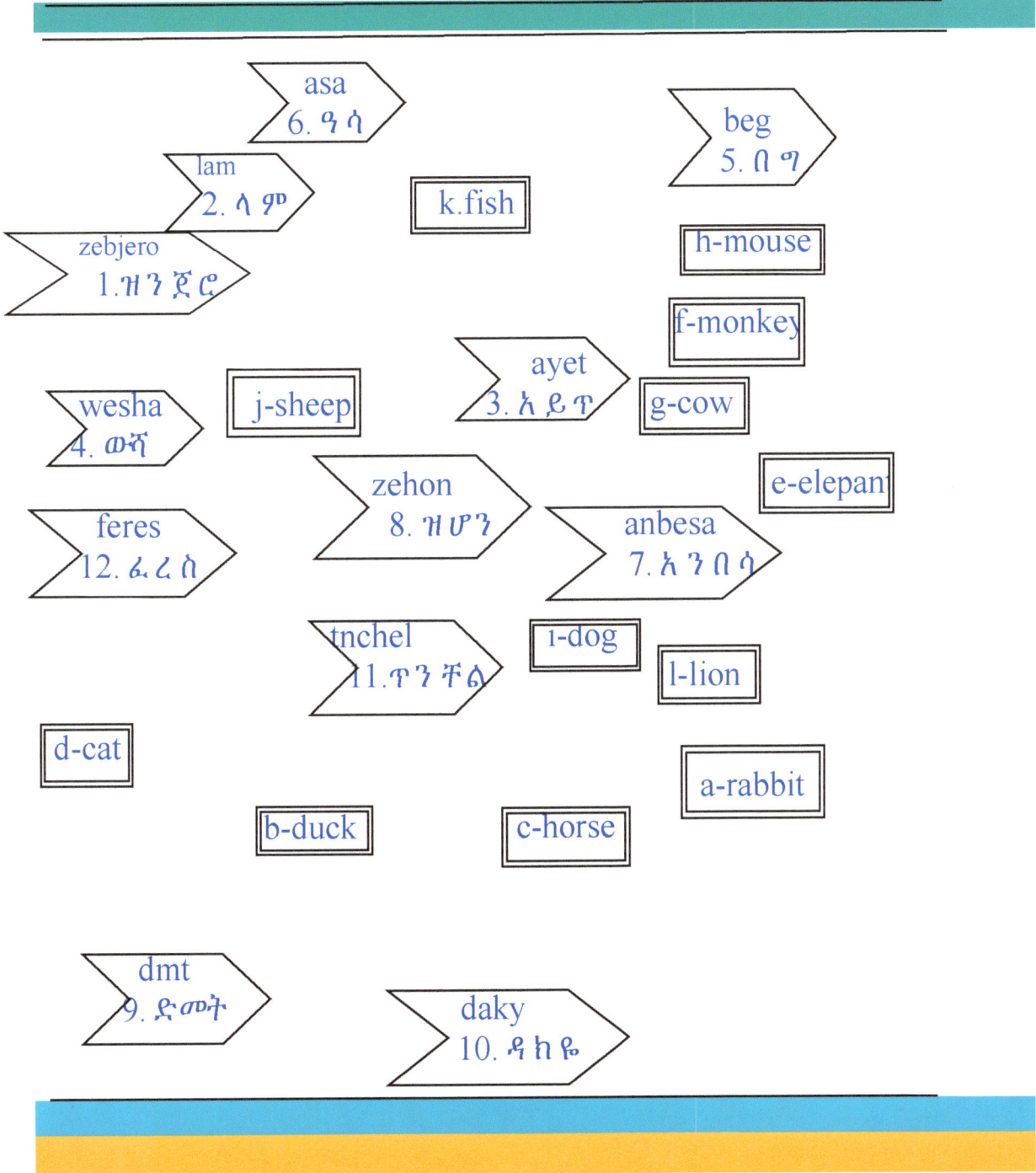

ገጽ/page 77

Match the animals to their associated pictures.

As in the example:

1. ላም

1.
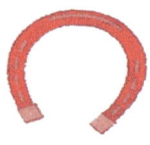

2. ፈረስ

2.

3. ድመት

3.

4. ጥንቸል

4.

Mixed word exercises

Look at the pictures and their meanings.

1. ጉንዳን/gundan-ant

2. ቢራ ቢሮ/birabiro-butterfly

Cont.....pronunciations and their meanings.

3. አሳማ/asama-pig

4. ሸረሪት/shererit-spider

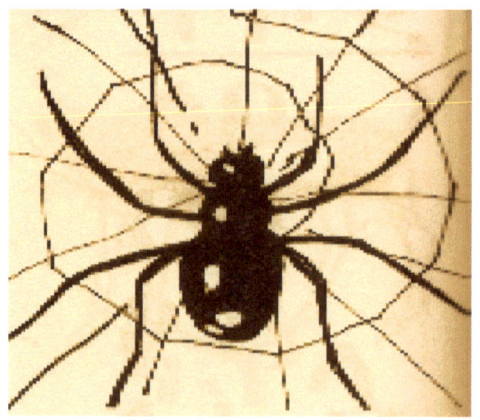

Cont.....pronunciations and their meanings.

5. ዝንብ/zenb-fly

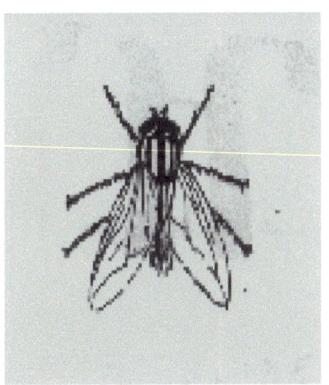

6. ትንኝ/teng-bug

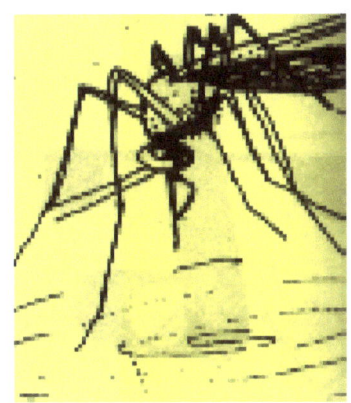

Mixed word exercises

Look at the Amharic words to English meanings and their pronunciations.

1. ያልጋ ልብስ/yalga lebes-bedspread

2. ፖስታ ቤት/posta bet-post office

3. ቴምበር/tember-stamp

4. ኳስ/ kuws-ball

5. ቀለበት/kelebet-ring

6. ወርቅ worq-gold

7. አልማዝ/alemaz-diamond

8. እንቁ/enqu-precious stone

9. ብር/berr-siliver

10. አንባር/anbar-bracelet

dialog

1. ሲኒማ ቤት ፊልም ይታያል
    Cinama bet film yetayal
    At a theater, you watch a movie.

2. ሰናይት ምግብ ሠራች
    Senayt megeb serach
    Senayt made/prepared food.

3. ከተማ ልሄድ ነው
    Ketma lehed now
    I will be going to the city;

Look at the pictures and their meanings.

1 ላም ስትታለብ/lam setetaleb-milking cow

2. ቅጠላ ቅጠል/qetela qtel-herbs

Look at the pictures and their meanings.

3, እንቁራሪት/ enqurarit-frog

4. በሬዎች/berywoch-bulls

Look at the pictures and their meanings.

5.ዶሮች/doroch-chichens

6.በጎች/begoch-sheep

Cont…. meanings.

7. **የፈረስ ቤት**/yeferes bet-stables

8. **የከብት ማርቢያ**/yekebet-animal farm

Cont….. their meanings.

9. ፍየል ከነ ግልገሉዋ/ feyel ken gelegeluwa-goat with kid

10. አውራ ዶሮ/awra doro-rooster

Cont…..their meanings.

11. አሳማ/asama-pig

12. ግመል/gmel-camel

Look at Amharic numbers

row/ተራ	Arabic-Amharic numbers አረብኛ ና አማርኛ ቁጥር	pronunciation አናባቢ	Amharic አማርኛ
1	1 one ፩	Aned	አንድ
2	2 two ፪	hulet	ሁለት
3	3 three ፫	soset	ሦሥት
4	4 four ፬	arat	ዓራት
5	5 five ፭	amest	አምስት
6	6 six ፮	sedeset	ስድስት
7	7 seven ፯	sebat	ሰባት
8	8 eight ፰	sement	ስምንት
9	9 nine ፱	zetegn	ዘጠኝ
10	10 ten ፲	aser	አስር

1-፩ 2-፪ 3-፫ 4-፬ 5-፭ 6-፮ 7-፯ 8-፰ 9-፱ 10-፲
20/፳ 30/፴ 40/፵ 50/፶ 60/፷ 70/፸ 80/፹ 90/፺ 100/፻

Look at Amharic numbers and learn how to count

row/ተራ	አርብኛ ቁጥር Arabic number-	አማርኛ ቁጥር Amharic number	አናባቢ pronunciation	በአማርኛ Amharic word
1	20	፳	haya	ሃያ
2	30	፴	selasa	ሰላሳ
3	40	፵	areba	አርባ
4	50	፶	hamsa	ሃምሳ
5	60	፷	selsa	ስልሳ
6	70	፸	seba	ሰባ
7	80	፹	semaniya	ሰማንያ
8	90	፺	zetena	ዘጠና
9	100	፻	meto	መቶ
10	1000	፼	And shi	አንድ ሺ

See if you can find these words in the word box.

The words can run left to right or top to bottom.

1. በሬ/berey
2. ጦጣ/Totah
3. በግ/beg
4. ጥጃ/teja
5. እንቁራሪት/ enqurarit
6. ላም/lam
7. ዶሮ/doro
8. ጥንቸል/tenchel

	1	2	3	4	5	6	7	8
1	በ	ግ	ጦ	ጥ	እ	ላ	ዶ	ፉ
2	ግ	በ	ጣ	ጃ	በ	ም	ሮ	ካ
3	ጥ	ጥ	ን	ቸ	ል	እ	ላ	ም
4	በ	ጃ	ላ	እ	ዳ	ን	ን	በ
5	ጥ	ጃ	ም	ን	ፉ	ቁ	ጥ	ሬ
6	ጃ	እ	ን	ቁ	ራ	ሪ	ት	ጠ
7	እ	ን	ቁ	ራ	ሪ	ት	ቤ	ዶ
8	መ	ዶ	ሮ	ጥ	ጃ	ል	ብ	ሮ

ክፍል ፪
Part Two

ክፍል ሁለት/Part Two

የቤት ዕቃ/Home Items

Look at the pictures of things you might see in a home.

1. ጠረጴዛ/terebeza

2. ወንበር/wonber

Cont…. might see in a home.

3. ስልክ/selk

4. መስኮት/meskot

Cont…. might see in a home.

5. **ቁምሳጥን**/qumsatn

6. **ቴሌቪዥን** television

Cont…. might see in a home.

7. **ማቀዝቀዣ**/maqezqqezja

8. **ምደጃ**/medeja

Cont.... might see in a home.

9. ፎቶ/photo

10. ምስል/seal

Cont.... might see in a home.

11. ሰዓት/seat

12. ሶፋ/sofa

Cont.... might see in a home.

13. a/ ያልጋ ልብስ yalga lebs-bedsppread

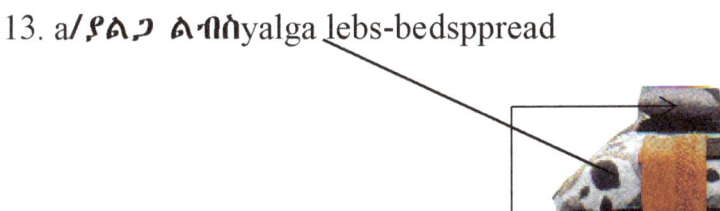

13 b. ትራስ/ tras-pillow   13.c አልጋ alga

If you can remember all the words, match the Amharic to the Pronunciation.

1. terpeza   a. መስኮት
2. meskot   b. ምድጃ
3. wenber   c. ጠረጴዛ
4. alga   d. ሶፋ
5. medeja   e. አልጋ
6. qumsaten   f. ቁምሳጥን
7 sofa   g. ስልክ
8. seat   h. ሰዓት
9. selk   i. ያልጋ ልብስ
10. maqezeqezja   j. ወንበር
11. mebrat   k. ማቀዝቀዣ
12. yalga lebs   l. መብራት

Match the Amharic words to English words.

1.	clock	1.	ወንበር
2.	cupboard	2.	መስኮት
3.	chair	3.	ቁምሳጥን
4.	door	4.	ሰዓት
5.	window	5.	ሲኒ
6.	glass	6.	ውሃ
7.	water	7.	ብርጭቆ
8.	cup	8.	በር

Match the words and their pronunciation.

1.	ber	1.	ምድጃ
2.	meskot	2.	መስኮት
3.	selk	3.	በር
4.	alga	4.	ስልክ
5.	medja	5.	አልጋ
6.	qumsaten	6.	ኮፒውተር
7.	Computer	7.	ትራስ
8.	tras	8.	ቁምሳጥን

Look at the Amharic words to English definition and its pronunciation.

	Amharic / አማርኛ	Pronunciation / አናባቢ	Definition / ትርጉም
1	መብራት	mebrat	Light
2	ጠርጴዛ	terbeza	Table
3	ውንበር	wenber	Chair
4	ስልክ	selk	Phon
5	መስኮት	meskot	Window
6	ሰዓት	seat	Watch
7	ስዕል	seal	Picture
8	አልጋ	alga	Bed
9	ሶፋ	sofa	sofa/couch
10	ቁምሳጥን	qumsaten	Cupboard
11	ማቀዝቀዣ	maqezqezja	Refrigerator
12	ምድጃ	medeja	Stove
13	ቁምሳጥን የልብስ	qumsaten ye lebs	closet/
14	በር	ber	open door
15	መዝጊያ	mezegiya	Door
16	ሙሽራ	mushera	bride and groom
17	ሙዜ	muzey	bride maid & best-man
18	ድብ	db	bear
19	አውራሪስ	aweraris	rhino
20	ጥጃ	teja	calf
21	እሳት	esat	fire
22	ሠርግ	serg	wedding
23	ገንዘብ	genzeb	money
24	እንፋዋለት	efuwalet	steam
25	የተቀደደ	ye teqeded	tear open//ripoff

ገጽ/page 100

Look at the pictures and their meanings

1. ሙሽራ/mushra-bride

2. መብራት/mberat-light

Cont…. their meanings

3. መዝጊያ/mezgiya-door (closed)

4. ላም ከነ ጥጃዋ/lam ken tjewa-cow&calf

Cont.... their meanings

5. ድብ/db-bear

6. አውራሪስ/awraris-rhino

Find the Amharic words and their English pronounce.

1. terepeza   a. መስኮት
2. meskot   b. ምድጃ
3. wenber   c. ጠረጴዛ
4. alga   d. ወንበር
5. medeja   e. ሶፋ
6. qumsaten   f. አልጋ
7. sofa   g. ቁምሳጥን
8. seat   h. ስልክ
9. selk   I. ሰዓት
10. maqezeqezja   j. መብራት
11. meberat   k. ማቀዝቀዣ

Find the Amharic pronounced words and their English meanings.

1.	table	1.	wenber
2.	bed	2.	terepeza
3.	chair	3.	meberat
4.	light	4.	alga
5.	stove	5.	seel
6.	picture	6.	mdeja
7.	painting	7.	photo
8.	telephone	8.	maqezeqejza
9.	refrigerator	9.	selk
10.	watch	10.	ya alga lebs
11.	pillow	11.	seat
12.	bed spread	12.	tras

Now see if you can fill in the household words by putting circle on the correct Amharic words.

1.

1-1. ወንበር   1-2. አልጋ   1-3. ጠረጴዛ

2

2-1. ሶፋ   2-2. አልጋ   2-3. ቴሌቪዥን

Cont.... circle on the correct Amharic words.

3.

3-1. ወንበር 3-2. ሶፋ 3-3. ጠረጴዛ

4.

4-1. ጠረጴዛ 4-2. ወንበር 4-3. ቴሌቪዥን

Cont.... circle on the correct Amharic words.

5.

5-1. ወንበር   5-2. ሶፋ   5-3. መስኮት

6.

6-1. ቁምሳጥን   6-2. ጠረጴዛ   6-3. መስኮት

Decide where these household items should go or would be. Then find it and write the correct number in the given image.

1. አልጋ	2. በር	3. መስኮት
4. ወንበር	5. ኮምፒውተር	6. ስልክ
7. ማቀዝቀዣ	8. ምድጃ	9. ሶፋ
10. ጠረጴዛ	11. ቴሌቪዥን	*12. መብራት

as in the example.
መብራት/mberat. light

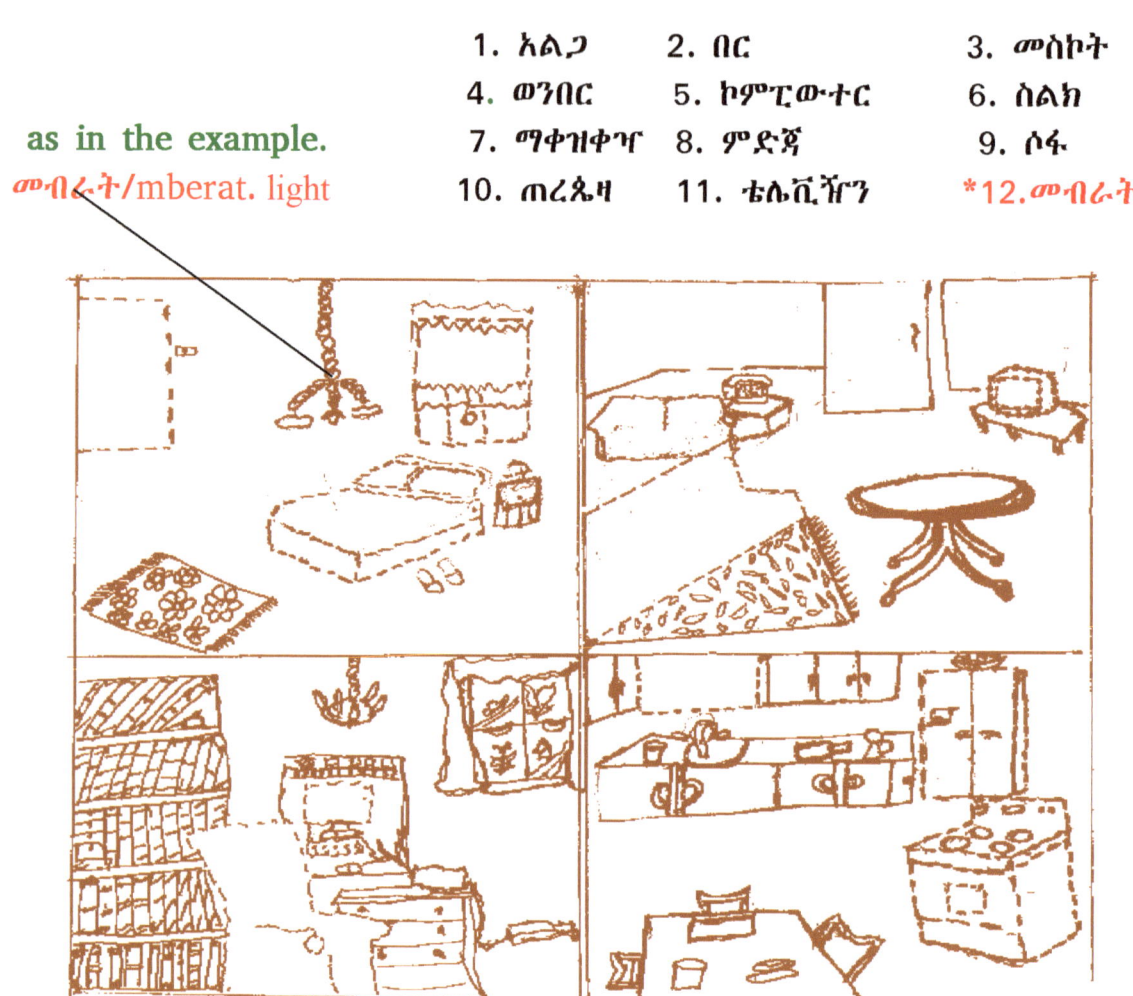

Exercises

1.	ber	1.	ምድጃ
2.	meskot	2.	መስኮት
3.	selk	3.	በር
4.	alga	4.	ስልክ
5.	mdeja	5.	አልጋ
6.	qumsaten	6.	ኮምፒውተር
7.	computer	7.	ቁምሳጥን

Connect the Amharic words to English means.

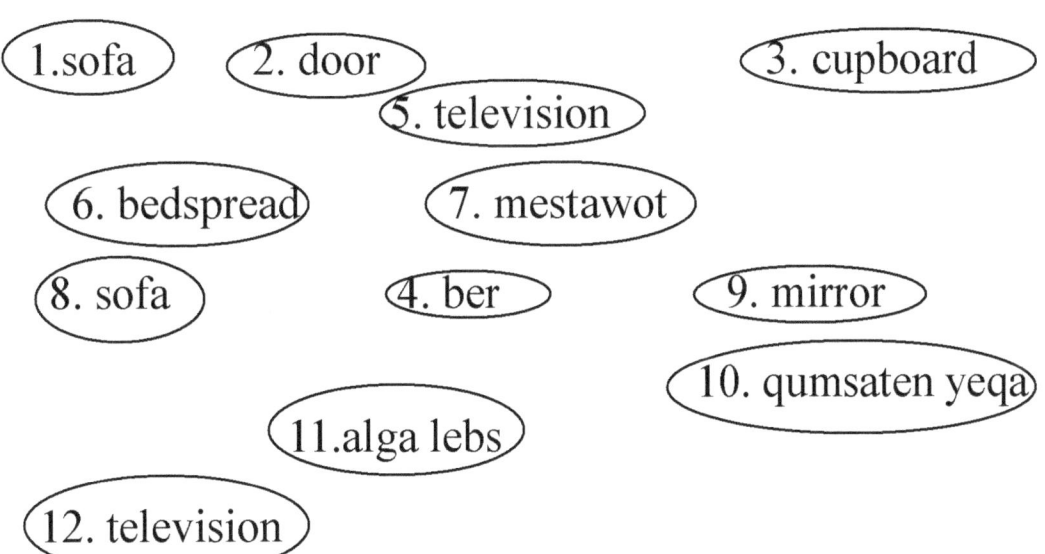

1. sofa 2. door 3. cupboard 5. television 6. bedspread 7. mestawot 8. sofa 4. ber 9. mirror 10. qumsaten yeqa 11. alga lebs 12. television

Decide where the house hold items should go. Then write the correct numbers in the picture, as in the example.

ምሳሌ/mesaley-example*6 ስልክ -e

1.	አልጋ-	2.	በር	3.	መስኮት	4.	ወንበር
5.	ኮምፒውተር	6*	ስልክ-e	7.	ማቀዝቀዣ	8.	ምድጃ
9.	ሶፋ	10.	ጠረጴዛ	11.	ቴሌቪዥን	12.	ስዓት

a. b. c. d

_____   -------   ----------   ----------

 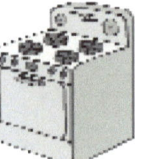  

*6e   f --------   g---------   h -----

i-------   j _____   k _____

l -------

ገጽ/page 111

Look at the Amharic words pronunciation and their meanings.

1. መቁረጥ/mequret-cut

2. መክፈት/mekefet-open

3. መቅዳት/meqedat-pour

4. የተቃጠለ/yeteqatel-burned

5. የተቀቀለ/yeteqeqel-broiled

6. የተጋገረ/yetegager-baked

7. ጭስ/ches-smocke

8. መጥበስ/metebes-fry

9. ማፍላት/mafelat-boil

10. ሊጥ/lit-dough

11. ማማሰል/mamasel-stir

12. መደባለቅ/medebaleq-mix

Mixed exercises
Match the Amharic words to their English meanings.

*example- 5. ብስክሌት/ bsklet-

1. መቁረጥ/mequret   1. dough

2. መክፈት/meketef   2. pour

3. መቅዳት/meqdat   3. cut

4. መጥበስ/metebes   4. stir

5. * ብስክሌት/bsklet ——————— 5. bicycle

6. ሊጥ/lit   6. fry

7. መደባለቅ/medebaleq   7. boil

8. ማማሰል/mamasel   8. chop

9. ማፍላት /mafelat   9. mix

10. መክተፍ/mktef   10. open

ልብሶች/lebsoch-clothes

Look at the picture of different clothes and their pronunciation.

1. ካፖርት/kaport-overcoat

2. ሹራብ/shurab-sweater

Cont…. their pronunciation.

3. ካልሲ/kalsi-socks

4 ቀበቶ/qebeto-belt

Cont.. . pronunciation.

5. ካኔተራ/kanetera-undershirt

6. ቁምጣqumta-short

Cont.. . pronunciation.

7. ቦርሳ/ borsa-bag

8. ሱሪ/suri-pants

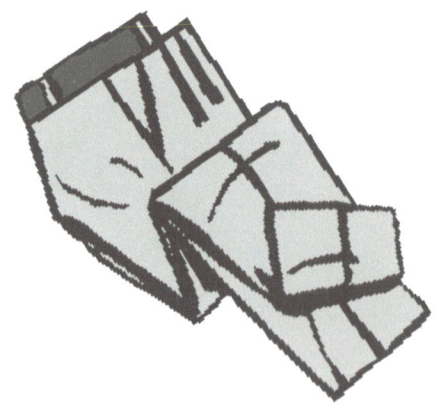

Cont... pronunciation.

10. ሸሚዝ/ shemiz-shirt

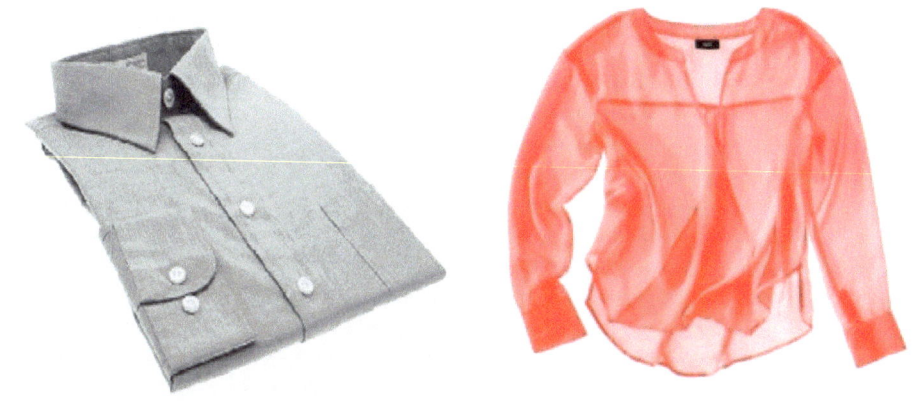

9. ጉርድ/gurd-skirt

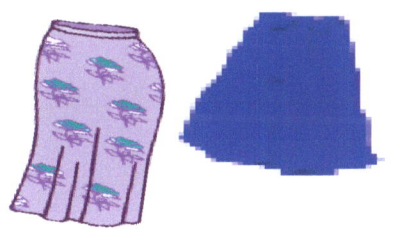

Cont... pronunciation.

11. ባርኔጣ/ barneta-hat

12. ቀሚስ/qemis-dress

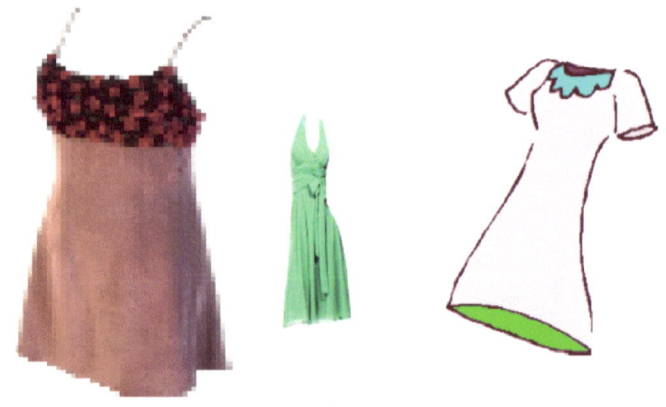

con... pronunciation.

13. ጫማ/chama-shoes

5. ጃኬት/jaket-jacket

Cont.... pronunciation.

15. የጅ ሹራብ yej shurab-gloves

16. መነፅር/menetser-glass

Cont.... pronunciation.

17. የቤት ጫማ/yebet chama-house shoes

Words on clothes and their associates
1. አንሶላ/ansola- bed sheet
2. ትራስ ልብስ/tras lebes-pillow cases
3. ሽቶ/sheto-perfume
4. ቅባት/qbat- any kind of cream or lotion
5. ፎጣ/fotah-towel
6. መሃረብ/mehareb-handkerchief
7. መርፌ/merfey-needle
8. መርፌ ቁልፍ/merfe qulf -safety pin
9. የገላ ሳሙና/yegela samuna-bath soap
10. ኩል/kul-eyeliner
11. መቀስ/meqes-scissors
12. ክር/ker-thread
13. ብሩሽ/Berush-brush
14. ጌጣ ጌጤ ማስቀመጫ/getageteh-nasqemecha- jeweler box
15. መቅረጫ/meqerech-sharpener
16. ሻሽ/shash –skarf
17. መቀንደቢያ/meqendebiya-tweezer
18. ጥፍር መቁረጫ/tefermequrecha-nail clipper
19. ጆሮ ማጸጃ/joro-matsedeja-ear swab
20. የጥፍር ቀለም/yetefer qelem-nail polish

Match the Amharic Words to their pronunciation.

1. ቀበቶ   a. shurab

2. ሹራብ   b. barneta

3. ካልሲ   c. chama

4. ሱሪ   d. kalsi

5. ጉርድ   e. qebeto

6. ባርኔጣ   f. kanetra

7. ጫማ   g. suri

8. ካኔቴራ   h. gurd

9. ሽሚዝ   I. Kaport

10. ቁልፍ   j. ybet chama

11. የቤት ጫማ   k. shemiz

12. ሻሽ   l. qulf

13. ካፖርት   m. shash

Find the missing Amharic alphabet words for clothes.

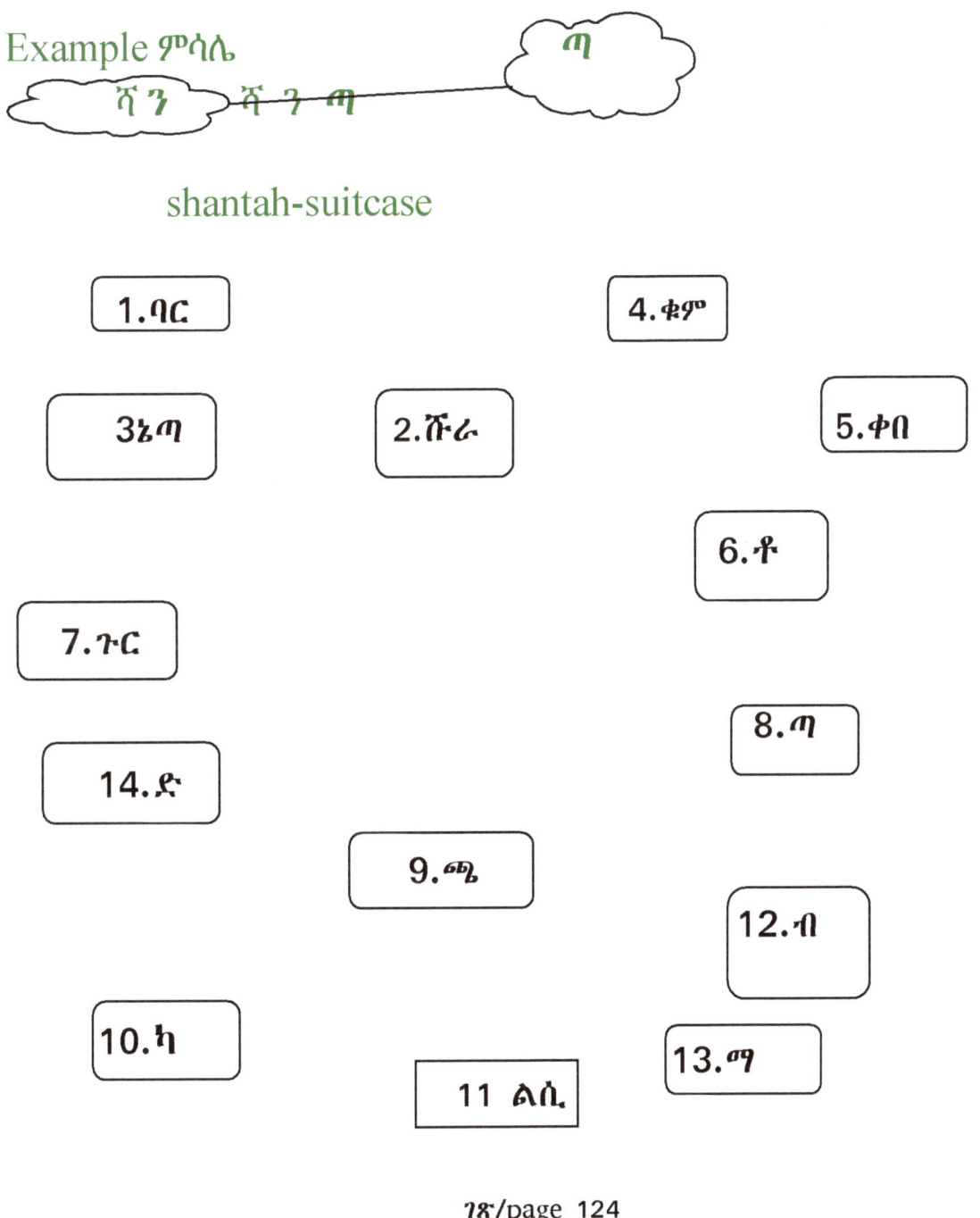

Example ምሳሌ

ሻንጣ

shantah-suitcase

1. ጋር
2. ሹራ
3. ጌጣ
4. ቀም
5. ቀበ
6. ቱ
7. ጉር
8. ጋ
9. ጫ
10. ካ
11. ልሲ
12. ቡ
13. ማ
14. ዱ

Match the Amharic Words to their pronunciation.

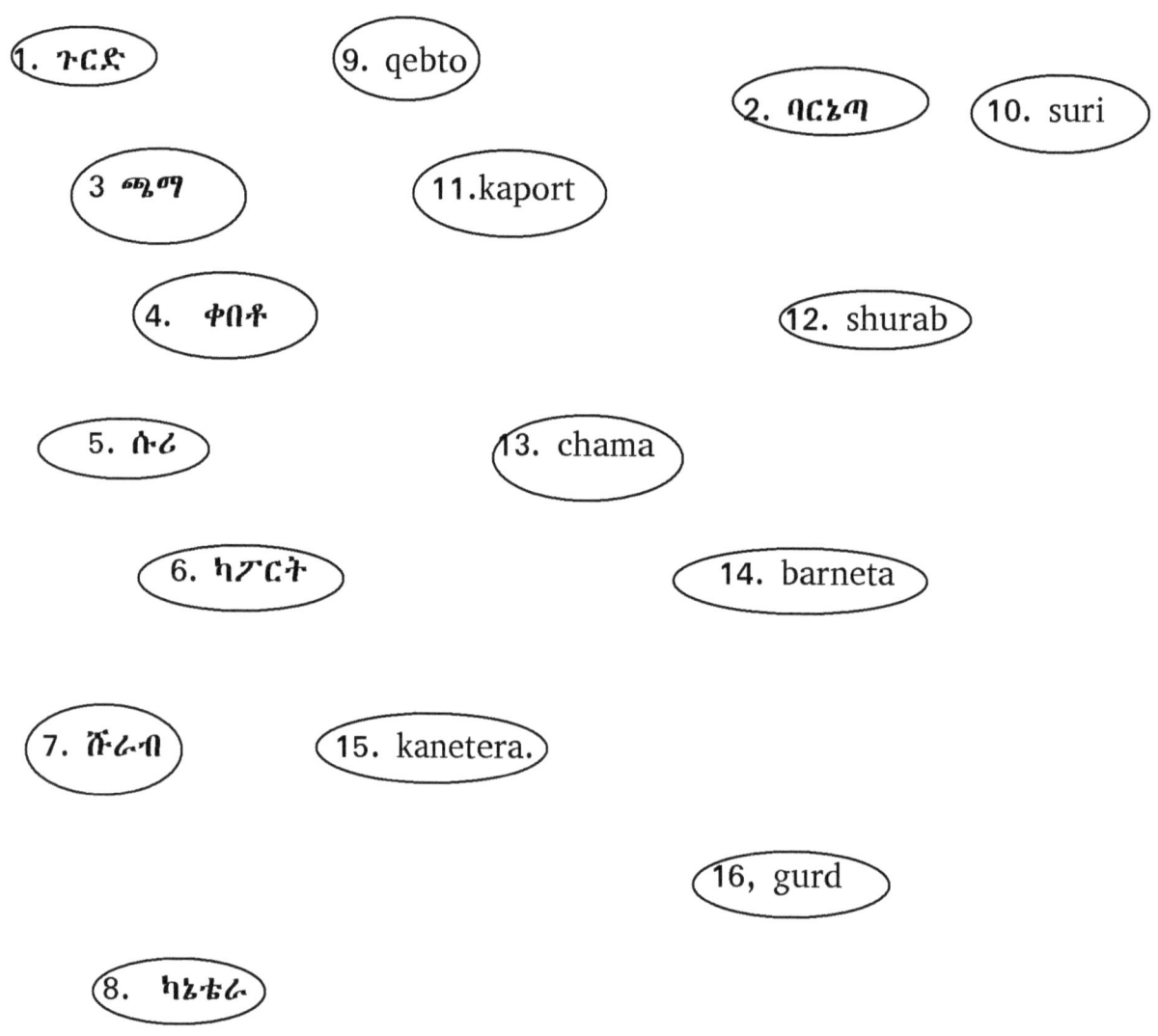

See if you can find these clothes in the word box.

1.   2.   3.   4.   5

6   7   8   9   10

11   12

	1	2	3	4	5	6	7	8
1	ቀ	በ	ቶ	ሱ	ሪ	ጬ	ማ	ካ
2	የ	ቤ	ሱ	ሪ	ባ	ማ	ኮ	ል
3	ኮ	ት	ሪ	ጉ	ር	ድ	ት	ሴ
4	ቀ	ሚ	ስ	ር	ኔ	ኮ	ባ	ቀ
5	ሹ	ራ	ብ	ድ	ጣ	ሹ	ር	በ
6	ጬ	ማ	ቁ	ም	ጣ	ራ	ኔ	ቶ
7	የ	ቤ	ት	ጬ	ማ	ቀ	ሚ	ስ
8	ፉ	ኮ	ት	የ	ቤ	ት	ጬ	ማ

ገጽ/page 126

Babule is going on vacation; count how many of each type of clothing she is packing in her suitcase,

፩-1 ማስታወሻ ደብተር___ ፪-2 ሻንጣ___ ፫-3 ቀበቶ___
፬-4 ሹራብ___ ፭-5 ጫማ___ ፮-6 ጉርድ___
፯-7 ቦርሳ___ ፰-8 ካልሲ___ ፱-9 ቀሚስ___
፲-10 ቁምጣ___ ፲፩-11 መነፅር___ ፲፪-12 የቤት ጫማ___
፲፫-13 ሱሪ___ ፲፬-14 ሻኝጣ___ ፲፭-15 ባርኔጣ___

ምግብ/megeb-food

Look at the picture of different foods and their meaning with pronunciation.

1. ፍራፍሬ/feraferey-fruits

2. አታክልት/ataklt-vegetables

ምግብ/megeb-foods

Cont.....pronunciations and their meanings.

3. ዳቦ/dabo-bread

4. ወተት/wetet-milk

ምግብ/megeb-foods

Cont.....pronunciations and their meanings.

5. እንጀራ/enjera-kind of tortilla it tests mild lime

6. ቂጣ/qita- like pancake Ethiopian has for breakfast it is Cranech.

ምግብ/megeb-foods

Cont.....pronunciations and their meanings.

7. ዘይት/ zeyt-oil

8. ሽንኩርት/shenkurt-onion

ምግብ/megeb-foods

Cont.....pronunciations and their meanings.

9. ቲማቲም/timatim-tomato

10. በቆሎ/bequlo-corn

ምግብ/megeb-foods

Cont.....pronunciations and their meanings.

11.ሎሚ/lomi-lemon

12.ሥጋ/sega-meat

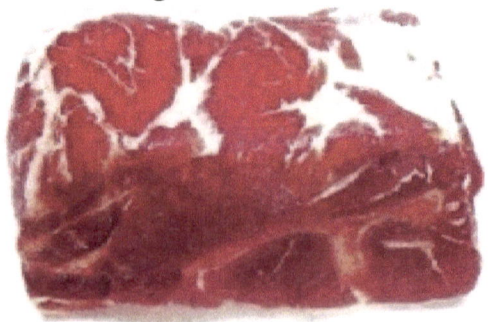

ምግብ/megeb-foods

Cont.....pronunciations and their meanings.

13. እንቁላል/enqulal-egg

14. አተር ክክ/ater kk-split pea

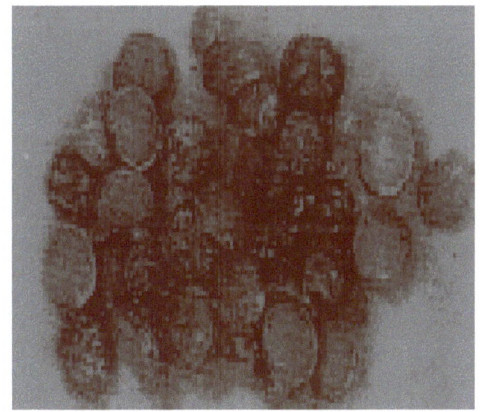

16. ምስር ክክ/mesre kk-split lentil

Cont.....pronunciations and their meanings.

15. ወጥ/wot Stew

17 ጨው/chew-salt

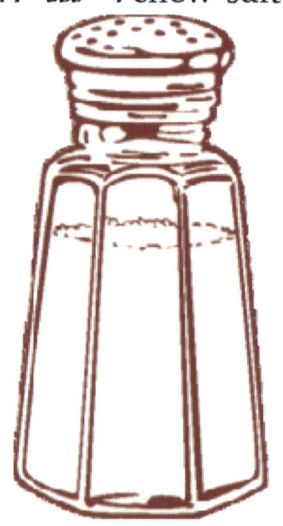

Cont.....pronunciations and their meanings.

18. ድንች/dench-potato

19. ነጭ ሽንኩርት/nech shenkurt-garlic

ምግብ/megeb-foods

Cont.....pronunciations and their meanings.

21. ቃሪያ/qariya-allkind of fresh peppers

22. ብርቱካን/bertukan/orange

Match the Amharic words to the pronunciation.

1	ዳቦ	a.	wotet
2	ዘይት	b.	dabo
3	ወተት	c.	zeit
4	እንጀራ	d.	atakelt
5	ፍራፍሬ	e.	enjera
6.	አታክልት	f.	feraferey
7.	ሥጋ	g.	lomi
8.	እንቁላል	h.	sega
9.	ብርቱካን	I.	Enqulal
10.	ሎሚ	j.	bertukan
11.	በቆሎ	k.	qariya
12.	ቃሪያ	l.	beqolo

* ተፈላጊ ቃል tefelagi qal /useful words

1. አባት/abat-father

2. እናት/enat-mother

3. እህት/ehet-sister

4. ወንድም/wendm-brother

5. አጎት/agot-uncle

6. አክስት/akest-aunt

7. ጓደኛ/ guwadnga-friend

8. ዘመድ/zemed-relative

9. እንጀራ አባት/enjera abat-stepfather

10. እንጀራ እናት/enjera enat-stepmother

11. የእህትና የወንድም ሴት ልጅ/yehet na yewendme set lej-niece

12. የእህትና የወንድም ወንድ ልጅ/ yehet na yewendme wend lej-nephew

13. የባል እህት/ምራት/ yebal ehet- merat= sister in-law (both side)

14. የባል ወንደም/አማች/ yebal wondem- amach=brother–in-law(both side)

15. የባል ወይንም የሚስት ወላጆች/አማት(አማቶች)
    yebal-wyem yemist welajoch-amat (amatoch) In Laws

* ተፈላጊ ቃል tefelagi qal /useful words

1. ጎረቤት/gorebet-neighbor
2. ገንዘብ ቤት/genzeb bet/cashier
3. ቤተ ክርስቲያን/betkerstiyan-church
4. መስጊድ/mesgid-mosq
5. ገዳም/gedam-monastery
6. መነኩሴ/menekusey-monk
7. መስቀል/mesqel-cross
8. ሻማ/shama-candle
9. መጥረጊያ/meteregiya-broom
10. እቅፍ/eqef-bench
11. መስታዎት/mestawot-mirror
12. መታጠቢያ ቤት/metatebiya bet-bathroom
13. እንግዳ ቤት/engeda bet-guesthouse
14. ፍርድ ቤት/fred bet-court
15. መኝታ ቤት/megnta bet-bed room

cont...*ተፈላጊ ቃል tefelagi qal /useful words.

1.	አንተ	ante	you(m)
2.	አንቺ	anchi	you(f)
3.	እናንተ	enante	you(plural)
4.	እኛ	egna	we
5.	በላ	bela	eat(m)
6.	ጠጣ	tehta	drank(m)
7.	ተኛ	tenga	slept(m)
8.	ተነሳ	tenesa	awake (m)
9.	እኔ	eney	me/I
10.	ተነሳች	tenesach	awake(f)
11.	ተኛች	tengach	slept(f)
12.	በላች	belach	eat(f)
13.	ጠጣች	tetahch	drank(f)
14.	እሱ	esu	him(m)
15.	አሱዋ	esuwa	her(f)
16	እነሱ	enesu	they (p)
17.	ይመጣሉ	yemetalu	will come (p)

cont...*ተፈላጊ ቃል tefelagi qal /useful words.

1. ሴት........................set/women
2. ወንድ.......................wond/man
3. ልጅ........................lej/child
4. ወንድ ልጅ...................wond lej/boy
5. ሴት ልጅ....................set lej/ girl
6. ጤና ይስጥልኝ/ሰላም
   tena yestlenge or selam............. good health to you. or
                                           peace/hello (both side)
7. አመሰግናለሁ ደህና ነኝ
   amesegenalehu dehena nenge.............thank you I am fine.
8. ስምህ ማነው?
   semeh manow?(m).....................what is your name?
9. ስሜ ማሞ ነው
   semey mamo now......................my name is mamo
10. ስምሽ ማነው ?
    semesh manow(f)...................... what is your name?
11. ስሜ ባቡ ነው
    semey babu now....................... my name is babu.
12. ወዴት ትሄዳለህ ?
    wedet tehedaleh?(m)....................where are you going?
13. ወደ ቤት
    Wodebet.....................I am going home.
14. ወዴት ተሄጃለሽ
    wedet tehejalesh?(f)....................where are you going?
    ወደ ሥራ
    Wodsera....................I am going to work.
15. እንደምነሽ?
    endemnesh?(f).............how are you doing?
        ደህና
    dehna ....fine.

cont...*ተፈላጊ ቃል tefelagi qal /useful words.

16. እንደምነህ ?
    endmeneh(m)..how are you doing ?
    ደህና
    Dehena.. fine

17. ስንት ሰዓት ነው
    senet seat now ?...................................what is the time?
    ከጠዋቱ ሶሥት(3) ሰዓት ነው
    ketewatu sost seat now........................9:00 am

(please note -Ethiopian uses time according day light rather than "am" and pm for example- (ketewatu arat 4 seat"means 10.00am)

18. ምሳ እንብላ
    mesa enbela ?......................................let's have lunch ?
    እሺ
    eshi.. okay

19. ቡና እፈልጋለሁ
    buna efelgalehu ....I want coffee?
    እሺ ቡና አፈላለሁ
    eshi buna afelalehu.......................... okay I will make coffee

20. ቁርስ ምን አለ?
    qurs meen ale? ....What do you have for breakfast?
    እንቁላል ጥብስ
    enqulale tebs ....fried egg

21. ሌላስ ምን አለ ለቁርስ?
    lelas meen ale lequrs? ....What else do you have for breakfast?
    የዶሮ ወጥ ፍርፍር
    yedoro wot ferer ....scramble enjera with chicken sauce

22. አመሰገናለሁ
    amsegnalehu ....thank you

23. ደህና ሁኑ
    dehena hunu..................good bye!

ክፍል ፫
Part Three

ክፍል ሦስት/Part Three
የሰውነት ክፍሎች /yesewnet kfloch-human body parts.

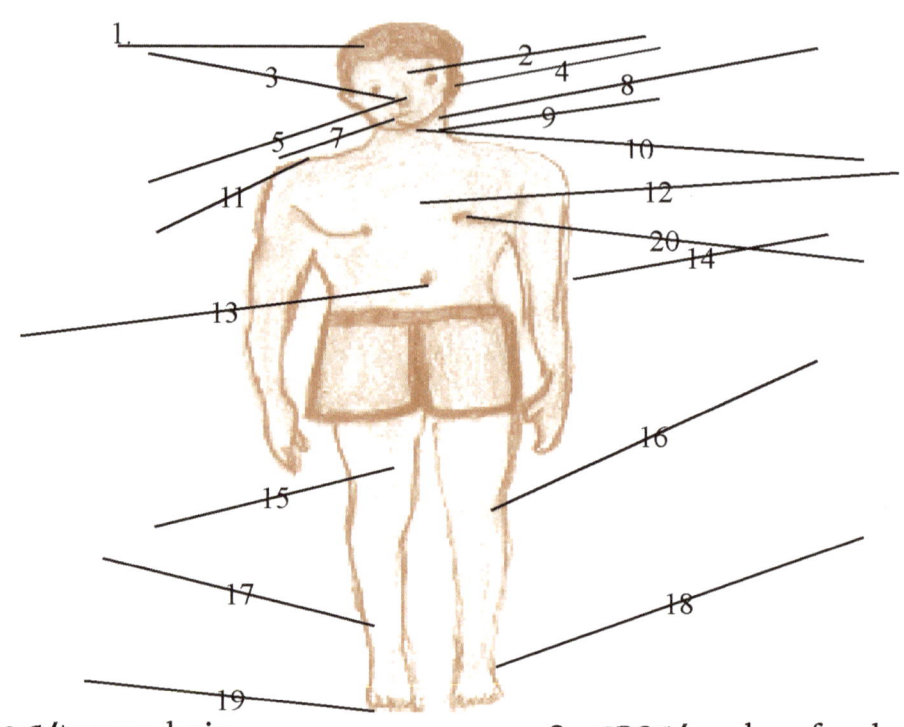

1. ፀጉር/tsegur-hair
2. ግንባር/genbar-forehead
3. ዓይን/ayn-eye
4. ጆር/joro-ear
5. አፍንጫ/afencha-nose
6. ጆሮገንድ/jorognd-jaw
7. አፍ/af-mouth
8. አገጭ/agech-chin
9. አንገት/anget-neck
10. ጉሮሮ/guroro-windpipe
11. ትከሻ/tekesha-shoulder
12. ደረት/dert-chest
13. እንብርት/enbrt-navel
14. ክንድ/kned-arm
15. ጭን/chn-thigh
16. ጉልበት/gulbet-knee
17. ቅልጥም/qltm-leg
18. ቁርጭምጭሚት/qurchmchemit-ankle
19. እግር/egr-foot
20. ጡት/tut-breast

የሰውነት ክፍሎች/ yesewnet kefloch - Human body parts.
Amharic words in human body parts meaning and their pronunciations.

፩-1 ፊት-fit-face

፪-2 ጥርስ-trs-teeth

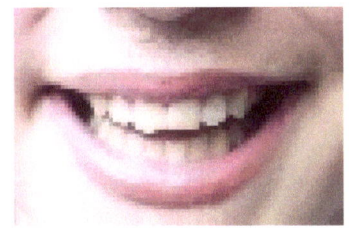

፫-3 ምላስ-mlas-tongue

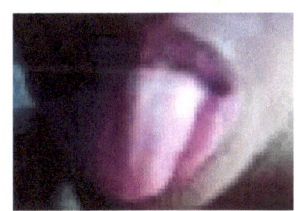

Look at the pictures of human body parts.

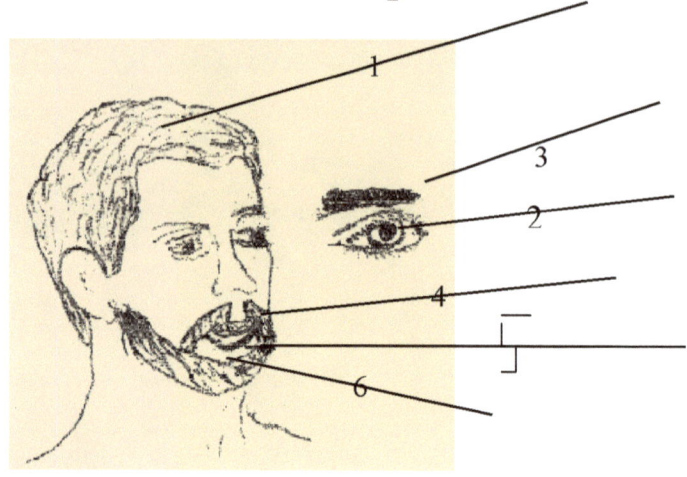

1. ራስ/ras-head
2. ሽፋል/shefal-eyelash
3. ቅንድብ/qndb-eyebrow
4. ሪዝ/riz-mustache
5. ጢም/tim-beard
6. ከንፈር/kenfer-lip
7. እጅ/eje-hand
8. አውራ ጣት/awera tat-thumb
9. ጥፍር/tfr-nail
10. የጥፍር ቀለም/yetfr qelem-
                      nail polish

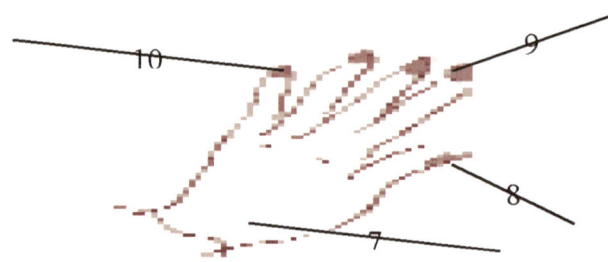

Amharic words in human body parts meaning and their pronunciations.

1. ክርን/krn-elbow
2. ቂጥ/qit-buttocks
3. ተረከዝ/terkez-heel
4. የግር አውራ ጣት/yegr awera tat-big toe
5. ብብት /bbt-armpit
7. ጣት/tat-finger

የሰውነት ክፍሎች/ yesewnet kfloch- human body parts.

Amharic words in human body parts meaning and their pronunciations.

1. አፍንጫ/afncha-nose
2. ክንድ/knd-arm
3. ዓይን/ayn-eye
4. ጣት/tat-finger
5. ራስ/ras-head
6. ጀርባ/jerba-back
7. ሆድ/hod-abdomen
8. እጅ/ej-hand
9. ጆሮ/joro-ear
10. ፀጉር/stegur-hair
11. ከንፈር/kenfer-lip
12. ጥርስ/trs-tooth
13. ግንባር/gnbar-forehead
14. አፍ/af-mouth
15. ፊት/ fit-face
16. ፈስ/fes- fart
17. ሽንት/shent-urine
18. አር/ar-feces
19. ላብ/lab-sweat
20. ቅርናት/qernat-odor

Match the Amharic words to English meanings

1. ras-head
2. tsegur-hair
3. genbar-forehead
4. gunech-cheek
5. angt-neck
6. agech-chin
7. tekesha-shoulder
8. deret-chest
9. kend-arm
10. ej-hand
11. hod-abdomen
12. wegb-waist
13. gulbet-knee
14. chn-lap
15. keltem-leg
16. egr-foot
17. yegr tatoch-toes
18. qurchmchemit-ankle
19. yegr awra tat-big toe
20. fit-face

1. ጸጉር
2. ራስ
3. አንገት
4. ጉንጭ
5. አገጭ
6. ግንባር
7. ክንድ
8. እጅ
9. ሆድ
10. ወገብ
11. ጉልበት
12. ጭን
13. ቅልጥም
14. እግር
15. ቁርጭምጭሚት
16. የግር አውራ ጣት
17. ደረት
18. የግር ጣቶች
19. ፊት
20. ትክሻ

Find and circle six parts of human body in the square and then draw them in the boxes below.

The words can run left to right and top to bottom.

ምሳሌ/example

ፊት/fit-face

Fill out the missing Amharic alphabets for human body parts.

1. አይ.   a. ፉ
2. አፍ..   b. ነፈር
3. አ.   c. ር
4. ከ...   d. ነጭ
5. ጄ.   e. ን
6. ሩ.   f. ግር
7. እ.   g. ርስ
8. ጠ..   h. ት
9. ፊ.   i. ጉር
10. አን..   j. ጅ
11. እ..   k. ገት
12. ጥ..   l. ስ
13. ቁርጭ....   m. ረከዝ
14. ተ...   n. ረት
15. ደ..   o. ምጭሚት

Look at the pictures meaning and follow Amharic pronunciation.

1. አነር/aner-cheetah

2. ኤሊ/ali-tortoise

Cont... look at the pictures meaning

4.   ፈጣን/fetan-faster

5.   ቀርፋፋ/qerfafa-slow

Cont... look at the pictures meaning

6. ጌጥ/geteh-jewelry

6. ወንድ/wend-man

Cont.... meaning and pronunciation.

7. ሴት/set-woman

8. ቀላል/qelal-light

ገጽ/page 154

Cont... look at the pictures meaning

9. ከባድ/kebad-heavy

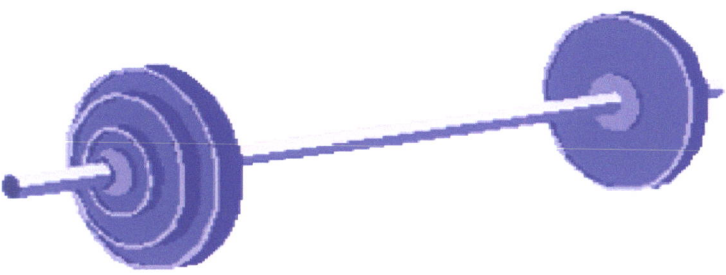

10. ወርቅ wood-expensive $1000.00

Cont... look at the pictures meaning

11.ርካሽ/rekash-cheap (99c)

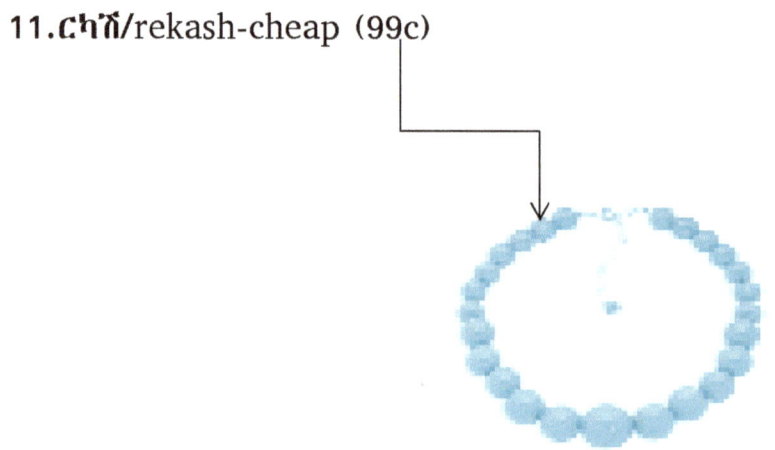

12. ትንሽ/tenesh-small   **13. ትልቅ**/telq-big

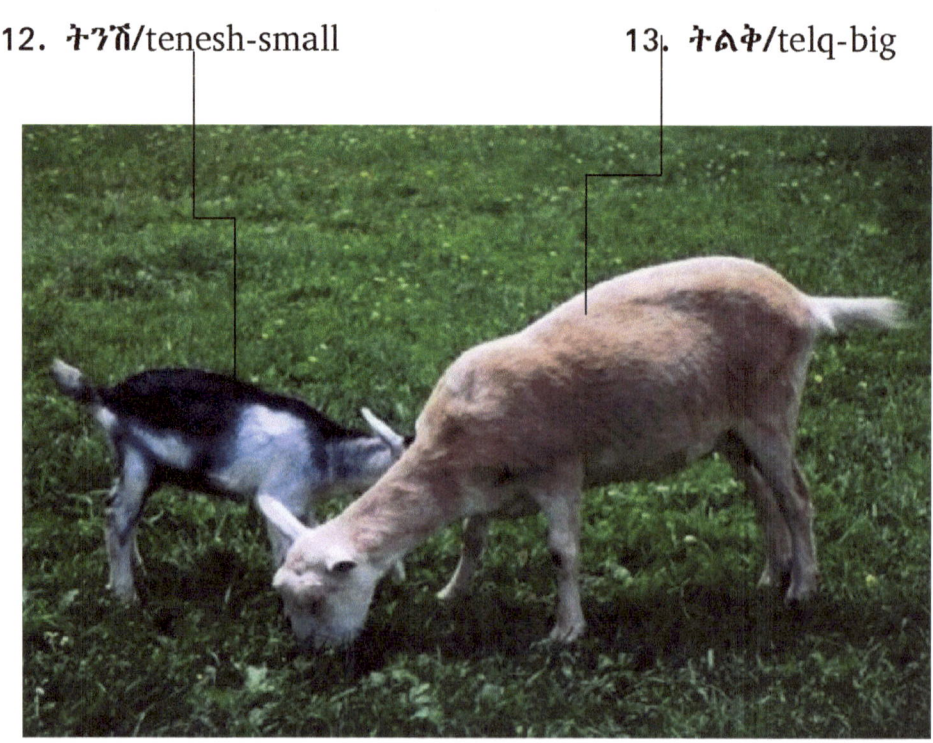

Choose the Amharic word that matches the picture and fill in the English word on the line by the picture or undeline it.

ምሳሌ/example   1a ውሻ/wesha   1b.በግ/beg   1c ዶሮ/doro

1b.በግ/beg-<u>sheep</u>

1.
99ሩ

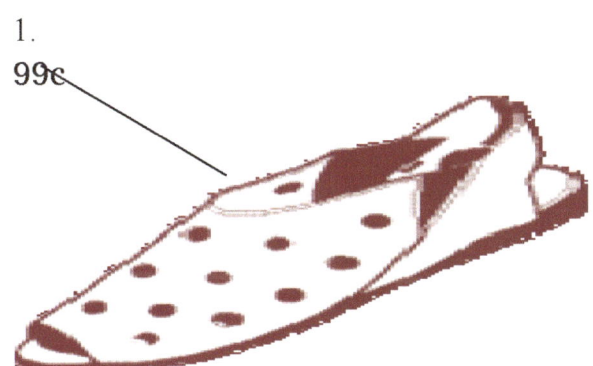

1a. ርካሽ/rkash   1b. ከባድ/kebad   1c. ፈጣን/fetan

Cont… underline it.

2.

2a ጌጥ/get   2b. ሰው/sew   2c. ከባድ/kebad

3.

3a. ጌጥ/geteh   3b. ጎታታ/gotata   3c. ሰው/sew

Cont… underline it.

4

4a. ፈጣን/fetan 4b. ከባድ/kebad 4c. አነር/aner

5.

5a. ርካሽ/rekash 5b. ፈጣን/fetan 5c. ጎታታ/gotata

Cont... underline it.

6.

6a. ከባድ/kebad   6b. ርካሽ/rkash   6c. ፈጣን/fetan

7a. አነር/aner   7b. ጌጥ/geteh   7c. ሰው/sew

Cont… underline it.

8

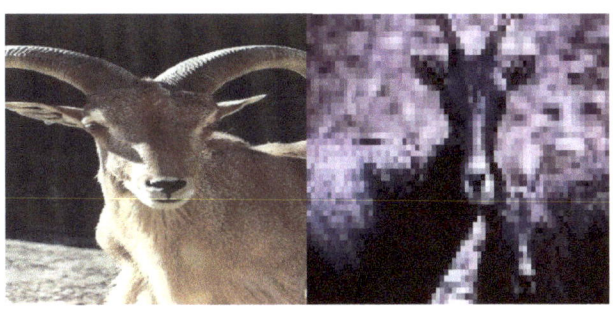

8a በግ/beg   8b. ፍየል/fyel   8c. ጥንቸል/tnchel

9

9a. አህያ/ahya-donkey   9b. ውሻ/wsha-dog   9c ዶሮ/doro-chicken

Cont… underline it.

10.

10a አውራ ዶሮ/awera doro-rooster 10b በግ/beg-sheep 10c ላም/lam-cow

11.

11a. ፍየል/fyel-goat 11b. ቀለበት/qelebet-ring 11c, አነር/ aner-cheetah

የሳምንቱ ቀናት/yesamnetu qenat
The Days of the week

Look at the days of the week and their Amharic pronunciation.

	በ አ ማር ኛ - In Amharic	Pronunciation	In English
1-፩	ሰኞ	Segno	Monday
2-፪	ማክሰኞ	Maxsegno	Tuesday
3-፫	ረቡዕ	Robue	Wednesday
4-፬	ሐሙስ	Hamus	Thursday
5-፭	ዓርብ	Areb	Friday
6-፮	ቅዳሜ	Qedamey	Saturday
7-፯	እሁድ	Ehud	Sunday

Dialogue

1.፩ ዛሬ ሰኞ ነው። zarey segno now
    Today is Monday.

2.፪ ነገ ምክሰኞ ነው።neg maxsegno now
    Tomorrow is Tuesday.

3.፫ ተነገዲያ ረቡዕ ነው። tenegodiya rebue now
    The day after tomorrow is Wednesday.

4.፬ ትናትና ሀሙስ ነበር። tenantna hamus neber
    Yesterday was Thursday.

5.፭ አርብ ማታ ስብሰባ አለ። areb mata sebsebs ale
    -Friday evening there is a meeting.

6.፮ ቅዳሜ ሠርግ አለ። qedamey serg ale.
    -on Saturday there is a wedding.

7.፯ እሁድ ጠዋት ቤተ ክርስቲያን እሄዳለሁ።
    ehud tewat bet kerstiyan ehedalehu
    -Sunday morning I will go to church

Find the Amharic words and connect it to their pronunciation.

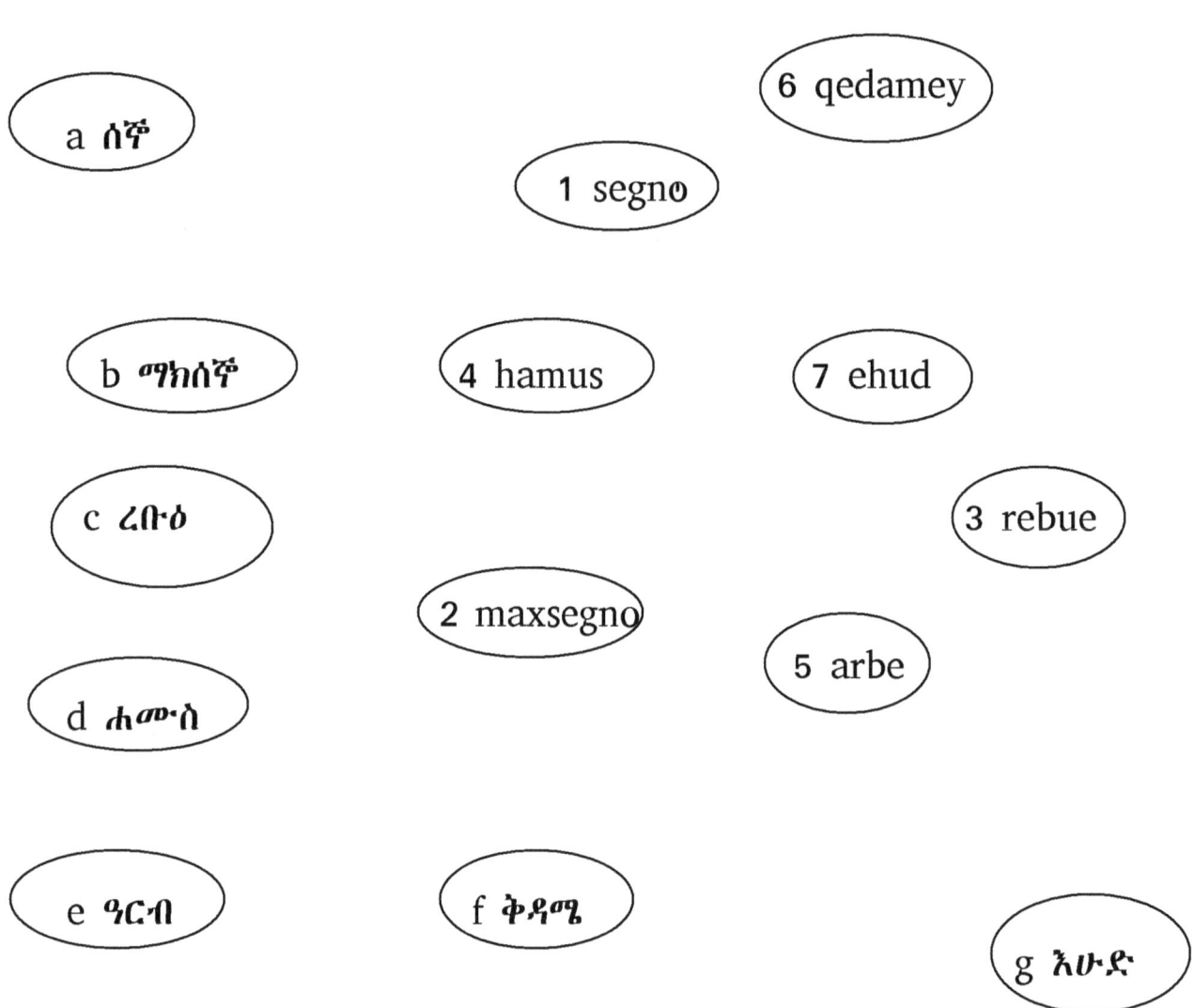

ወራት/werat-months

	በአማርኛ - In Amharic	Pronunciation	In English
1-፩	መስከረም	meskerem	September
2-፪	ጥቅምት	teqemt	October
3-፫	ህዳር	hedar	November
4-፬	ታህሣሥ	tahesas	December
5-፭	ጥር	ter	January
6-፮	የካቲት	yekatit	February
7-፯	መጋቢት	megabit	march
8-፰	ሚያዚያ	miyaziya	April
9-፱	ግንቦት	genbot	may
10-፲	ሰኔ	seney	June
11-፲፩	ሐምሌ	hamley	July
12-፲፪	ነሃሴ	nehasey	august
13-፲፫	ጳጉሜ	pagumey	Only 5&6 days

Match the months in Amharic words to their pronunciation.

1	meskerem-September	a	መጋቢት
2	hedar-November	b	ጥቅምት
3	yekatit-February	c	የካቲት
4	megabit-March	d	ግንቦት
5.	miyaziya- April	e	ህዳር
6.	teqmet-October	f	ሰኔ
7.	tahsas-December	g	መስከረም
8.	genbot-may	h	ሚያዝያ
9.	hamley-July	I	ነሃሴ-
10.	seney-June	j	ጥር
11.	nehasey-August	k	ጳጉሜ
12.	ter-January	l	ሐምሌ
13.	pagumey-pagumey	m	ታህሳስ

መለማመጃ/exercises

Write in Amharic all the months you think you know?

1_____ 2_____ 3____ 4_____ 5___ 6_____ 7_____

8_____ 9_____ 10___ 11_____ 12_____ 13____

Look at these Amharic word pronunciations and identify which word contains a month then write the word in the given space. If you do not find a month in the sentence, just put an X in the given space.

1. teqemet huletegnaw wor now._____
   ጥቅምት ሁለተኛው ወር ነው።

2. seney zenab ynoral._____
   ሰኔ ዝናብ ይኖራል።

3. qedamey ena ehud yereft gize now._____
   ቅዳሜ እና እሁድ የረፍት ጊዜ ነው።

4. pagumey yeametu mecheresha wor now._____
   ጳጉሜ ያመቱ መጨርረሻ ወር ነው።

5. sostengaw wor man yebalale?_____
   ሦሥተኛው ወር ማን ይባላል።

6. ye hulet weroch sem tsaf_____
   የሁለት ወሮች ስም ጻፍ።

7. ter sentegnaw wer now?_____
   ጥር ስንተኛው ወር ነው።

8. ledeteh/tesh yetegnaw wer lay now?_____
   ልደትህ/ሽ የትኛው ወር ላይ ነው።

9. hameley,nehasey yezeb werat now_____
   ሐምሌናነሃሴ የዘናብ ወራት ነው።

10. ye ehetey ledet be miyazya woost now _____
    የእህቴ ልደት በሚያዝያ ውስጥ ነው።

ቀለማት/Qelemat-Colors

Look at the colors and their Amharic meanigs and pronunciations.

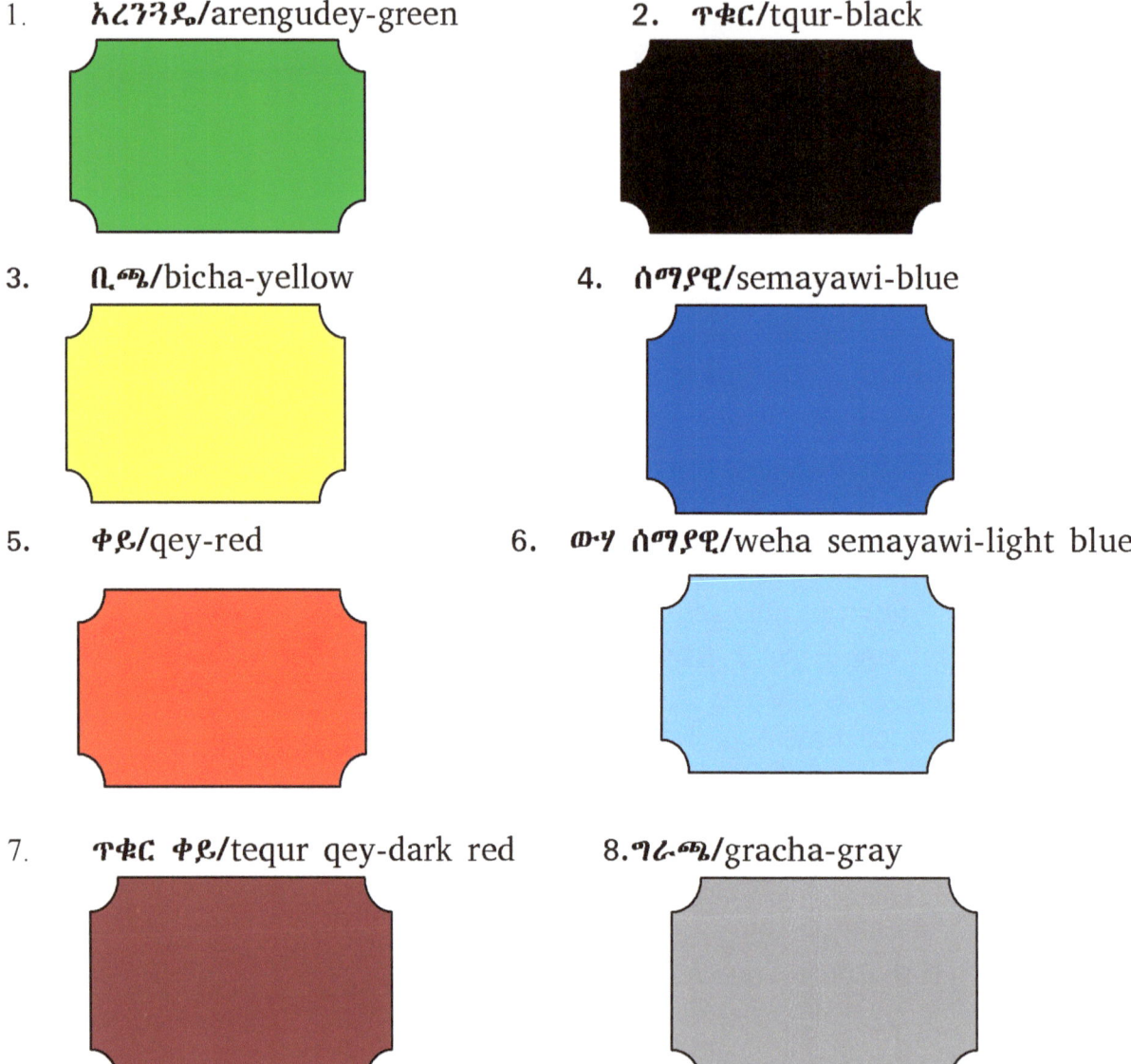

Note: *Due to printing outcome, colors may be slightly different.*

Cont... meaning and pronunciation.

9. ቡናማ/bunama-brown

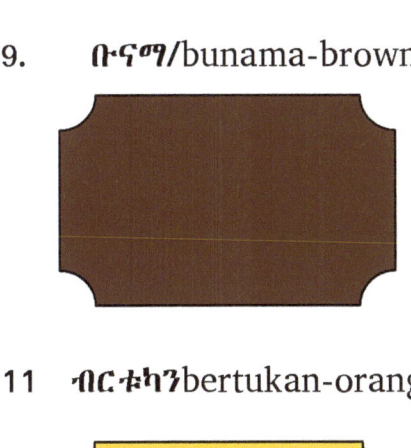

10. ብርማ/berma-siliver

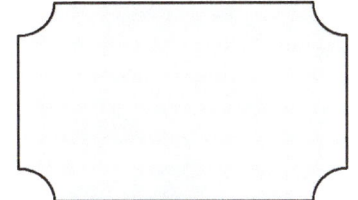

11. ብርቱካን/bertukan-orange

12. ነጭ/nech-white

13. ሃምራዊ/hamrawi-rose

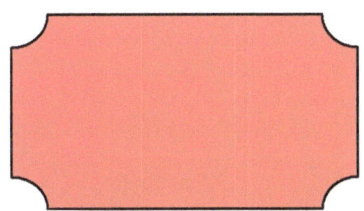

14. ወይን ጠጅ weyn tej-purple

15. ወርቅማ/werqma-gold

16. ውጥኔ/wetney-brighter orange

Note: *Due to printing outcome, colors may be slightly different.*

Cont.... meaning and pronunciation.

17. ጥቁር ሰማያዊ/tequr semayawi-dark blue

18. ነጣ ያለ ቢጫ/neta yal bicha-light yellow

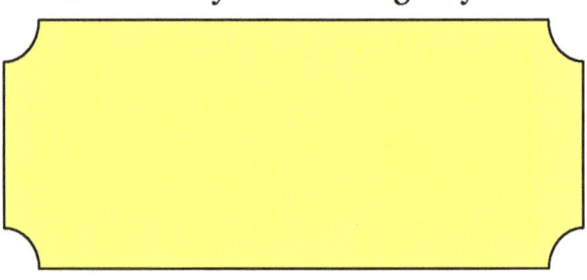

19. ነጣ ያለ ወይን ጠጅ/neta yal weyn tej-violet

20. ነጣ ያለ አረንጓዴ/neta yal arenguwadey-light-green

Note: *Due to printing outcome, colors may be slightly different.*

Match the Amharic word in color to English meaning.

1. ሰማያዊ/blue   a. hamerawi

2. ጥቁር/ black   b. bicha

3. ቀይ/red   c. wea semayawi

4. ሃምራዊ/rose   d. weyn tej

5. ቢጫ/yellow   e. bunama

6. አረንጓዴ/green   f. semayawi

7. ውሃ ሰማያዊ/light blue   g. tqur

8. ወይን ጠጅ/purple   h. nech

9. ቡናማ/brown   i. gracha

10. ብርማ/siliver   j. tqur qey

11. ነጭ/white   k. wteney

12. ብርቱካን/Orange   l. brma

13. ውጤ/bright orange   m. qey

14. ጥቁር ቀይ/dark red   n. arenguwadey

15. ግራጫ/gray   o. brtukan

Look at the colors of the flag and their Amharic pronunciations.

ኢትዮጵያ ባንዲራ/ Ethiopia   **የተባበሩት አሜሪካ ግዛቶች ባንዲራ/**U.S.A

1. **የኢትዮጵያ ባንዲራ ቀለማት** ye Ethiopia bandira qelemat
   Ethiopian flag colors are

a/ **አረንጓዴ/**arenguwadey- green
b/ **ቢጫ/**bicha-yellow
c/ **ቀይ**-qey- red **ናቸው/**nachew

2. **የአሜሪካን ባንዲራ ቀለማት/**ye American bandira qelmat
   American flag colors are

a/ **ነጭ/**nech-white
b/ **ቀይ/**qey-red
c/ **ጥቁር ሰማያዊ/**tequr semayawi-dark blue **ናቸው/**nachew

Find the Ethiopian and American Flag-color words in the box below. See how many new words you can find and log them.

ተራ/row	1	2	3	4	5	6	7	8	9
1	ቀ	ለ	ም	አ	ረ	ን	ኋ	ዮ	ከ
2	ነ	ጮ	ፐ	ራ	እ	ሜ	ር	ካ	ቢ
3	እ	ሰ	ቁ	ን	ማ	ኢ	አ	ቢ	ጬ
4	ፉ	ሜ	ር	ኋ	ቀ	ት	ሜ	ቀ	ይ
5	ሬ	ን	ሰ	ዮ	ይ	ዮ	ር	ም	ላ
6	ከ	ሏ	ማ	ራ	ኚ	ጹ	ከ	ስ	ት
7	ፈ	ላ	ያ	ላ	ጠ	ያ	ም	ሩ	ቅ
8	ሞ	ኝ	ዊ	ሰ	ሜ	ን	ፕ	ቅ	ፓ
9	ፕ	ቁ	ር	ስ	ማ	ያ	ዊ	ቀ	ይ
10	ነ	ቃ	ነ	ጮ	ባ	ን	ዲ	ሩ	ፕ

1 _____

2. _____

3. _____

4. _____

5. _____

ማመሳከሪያ

mamesakeriya

corroborate

ፊደል

ተራ	1	2	3	4	5	6	7
1	ሀ	ሁ	ሂ	ሃ	ሄ	ህ	ሆ
2	ለ	ሉ	ሊ	ላ	ሌ	ል	ሎ
3	ሐ	ሑ	ሒ	ሓ	ሔ	ሕ	ሖ
4	መ	ሙ	ሚ	ማ	ሜ	ም	ሞ
5	ሰ	ሱ	ሲ	ሳ	ሴ	ስ	ሶ
6	ረ	ሩ	ሪ	ራ	ሬ	ር	ሮ
7	ሠ	ሡ	ሢ	ሣ	ሤ	ሥ	ሦ
8	ሸ	ሹ	ሺ	ሻ	ሼ	ሽ	ሾ
9	ቀ	ቁ	ቂ	ቃ	ቄ	ቅ	ቆ
10	በ	ቡ	ቢ	ባ	ቤ	ብ	ቦ
11	ተ	ቱ	ቲ	ታ	ቴ	ት	ቶ
12	ቸ	ቹ	ቺ	ቻ	ቼ	ች	ቾ
13	ኀ	ኁ	ኂ	ኃ	ኄ	ኅ	ኆ
14	ነ	ኑ	ኒ	ና	ኔ	ን	ኖ
15	ኘ	ኙ	ኚ	ኛ	ኜ	ኝ	ኞ
16	አ	ኡ	ኢ	ኣ	ኤ	እ	ኦ
17	ከ	ኩ	ኪ	ካ	ኬ	ክ	ኮ
18	ኸ	ኹ	ኺ	ኻ	ኼ	ኽ	ኾ
19	ወ	ዉ	ዊ	ዋ	ዌ	ው	ዎ
20	ዐ	ዑ	ዒ	ዓ	ዔ	ዕ	ዖ
21	ዘ	ዙ	ዚ	ዛ	ዜ	ዝ	ዞ
22	ዠ	ዡ	ዢ	ዣ	ዤ	ዥ	ዦ
23	የ	ዩ	ዪ	ያ	ዬ	ይ	ዮ
24	ደ	ዱ	ዲ	ዳ	ዴ	ድ	ዶ
25	ጀ	ጁ	ጂ	ጃ	ጄ	ጅ	ጆ
26	ገ	ጉ	ጊ	ጋ	ጌ	ግ	ጎ
27	ጠ	ጡ	ጢ	ጣ	ጤ	ጥ	ጦ
28	ጨ	ጩ	ጪ	ጫ	ጬ	ጭ	ጮ
29	ጰ	ጱ	ጲ	ጳ	ጴ	ጵ	ጶ
30	ጸ	ጹ	ጺ	ጻ	ጼ	ጽ	ጾ
31	ፀ	ፁ	ፂ	ፃ	ፄ	ፅ	ፆ
32	ፈ	ፉ	ፊ	ፋ	ፌ	ፍ	ፎ
33	ፐ	ፑ	ፒ	ፓ	ፔ	ፕ	ፖ

ማመሳከሪያ/yemamesakeria-corroborate

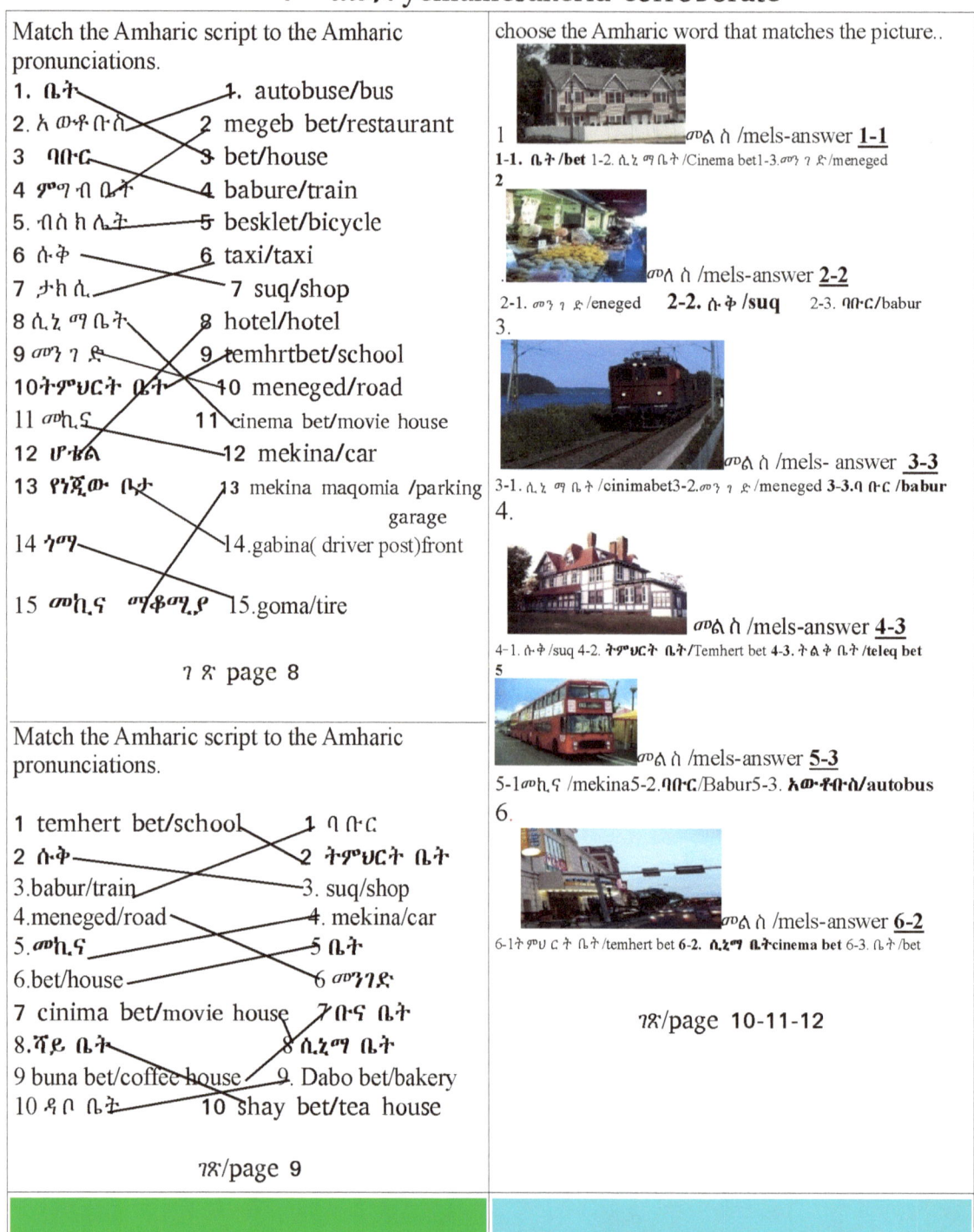

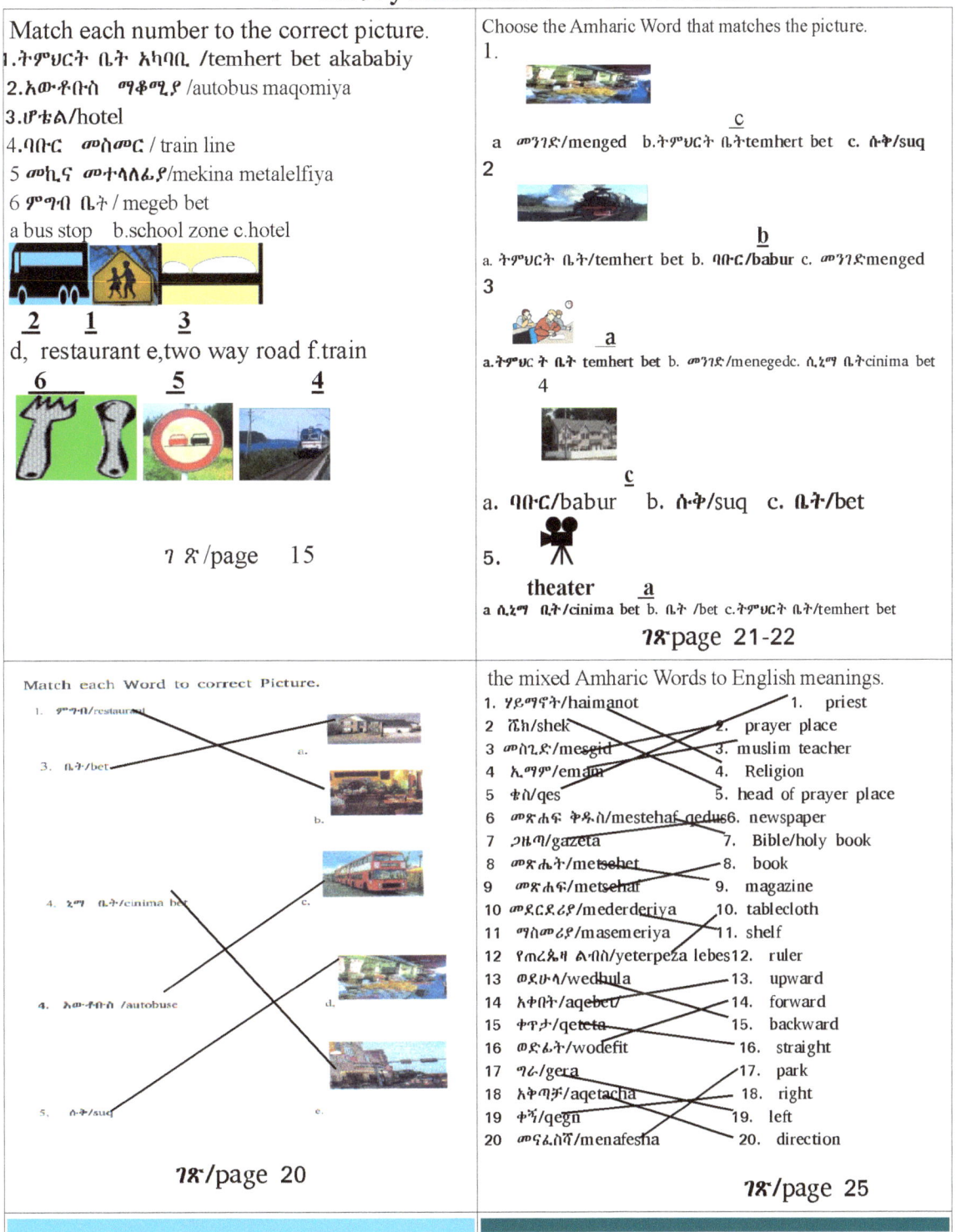

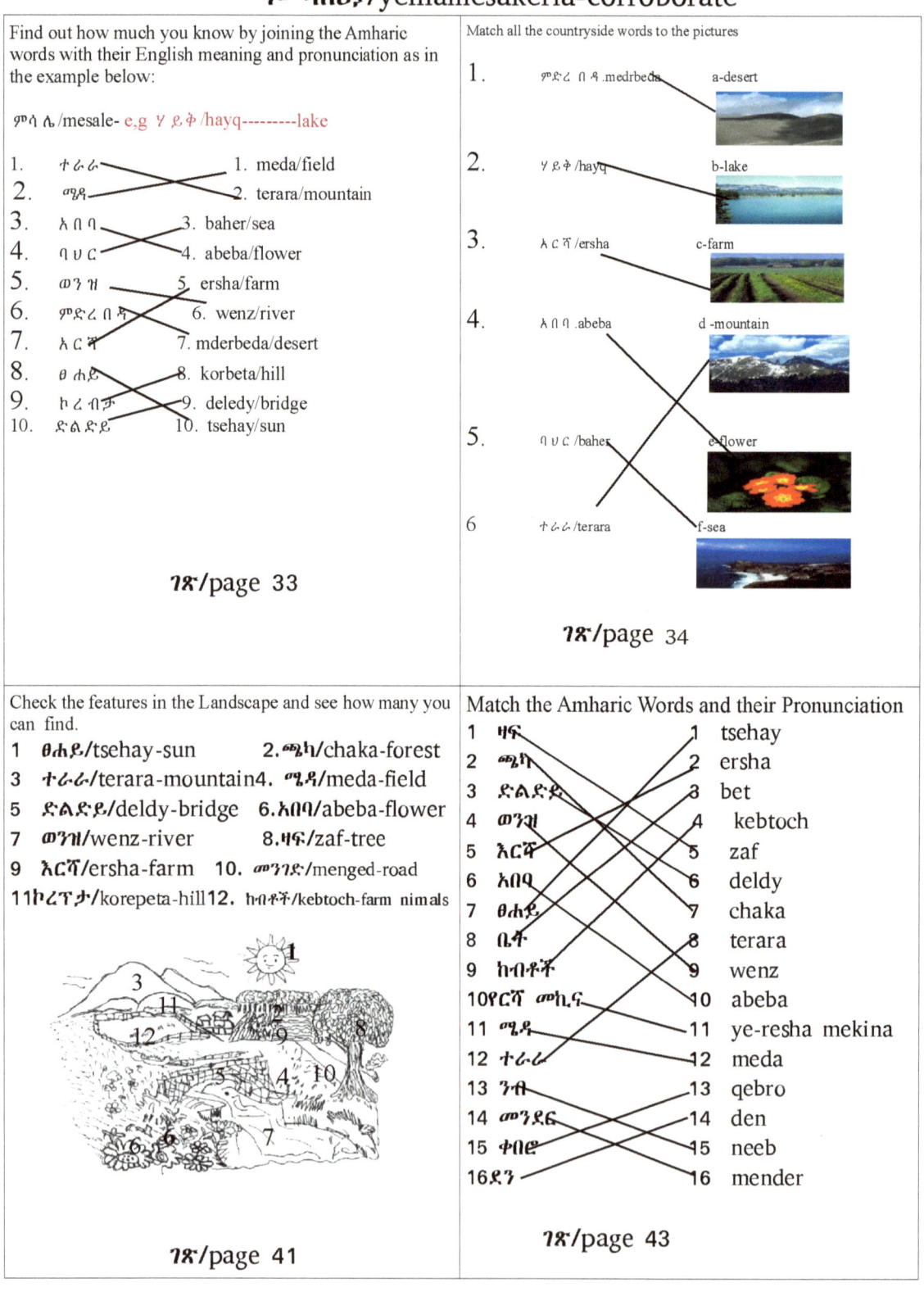

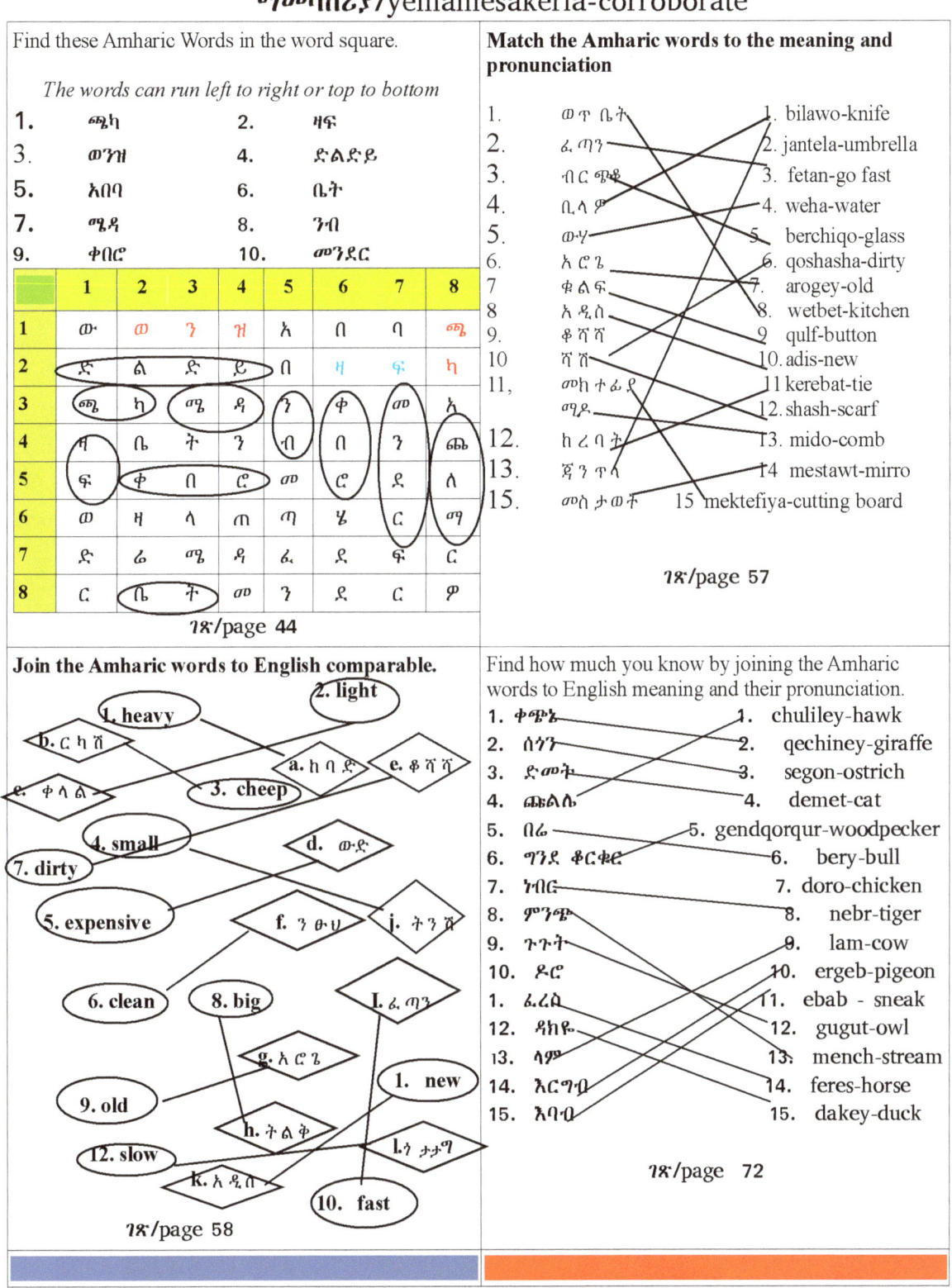

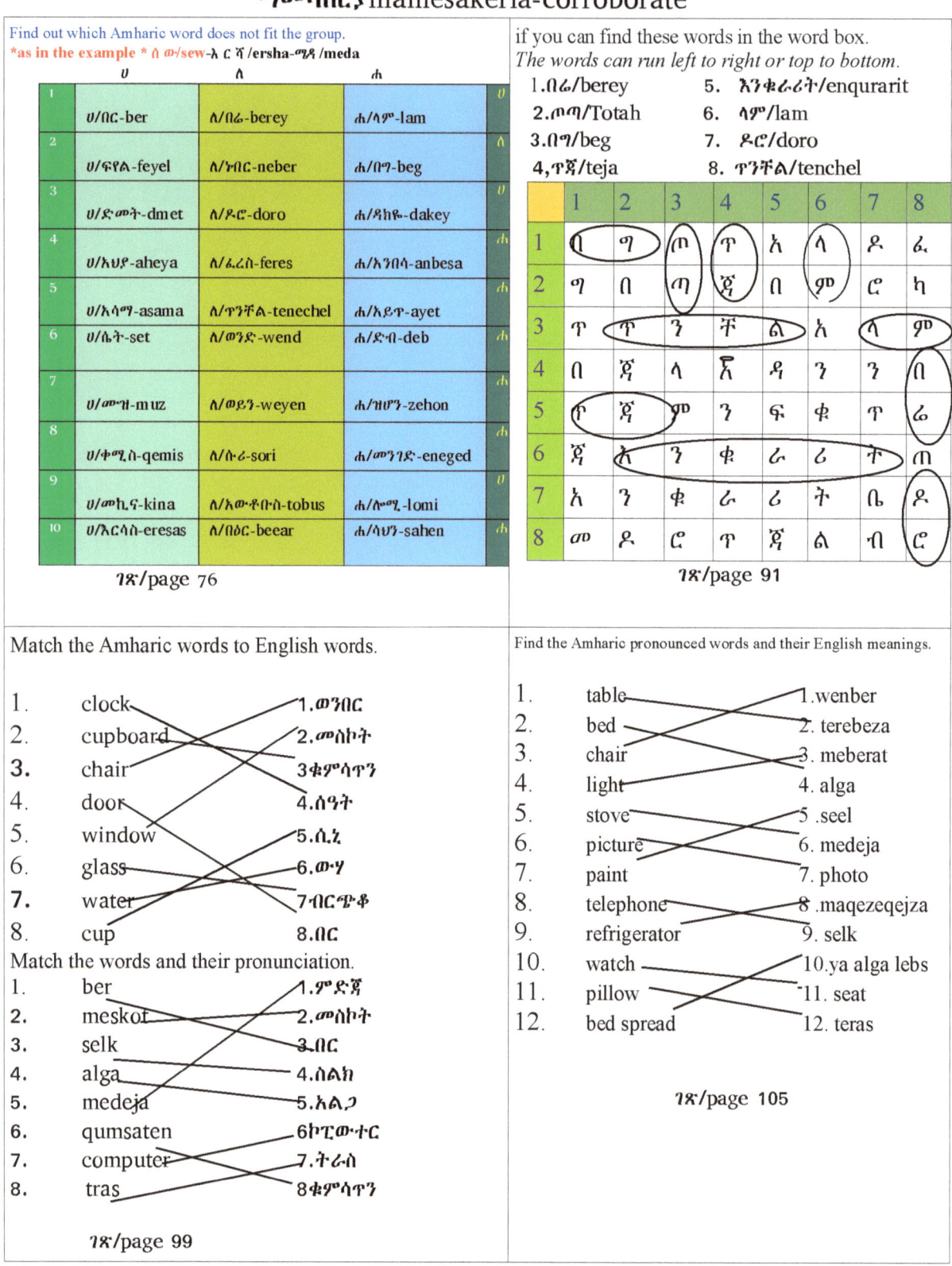

ማመሳከሪያ/yemamesakeria-corroborate

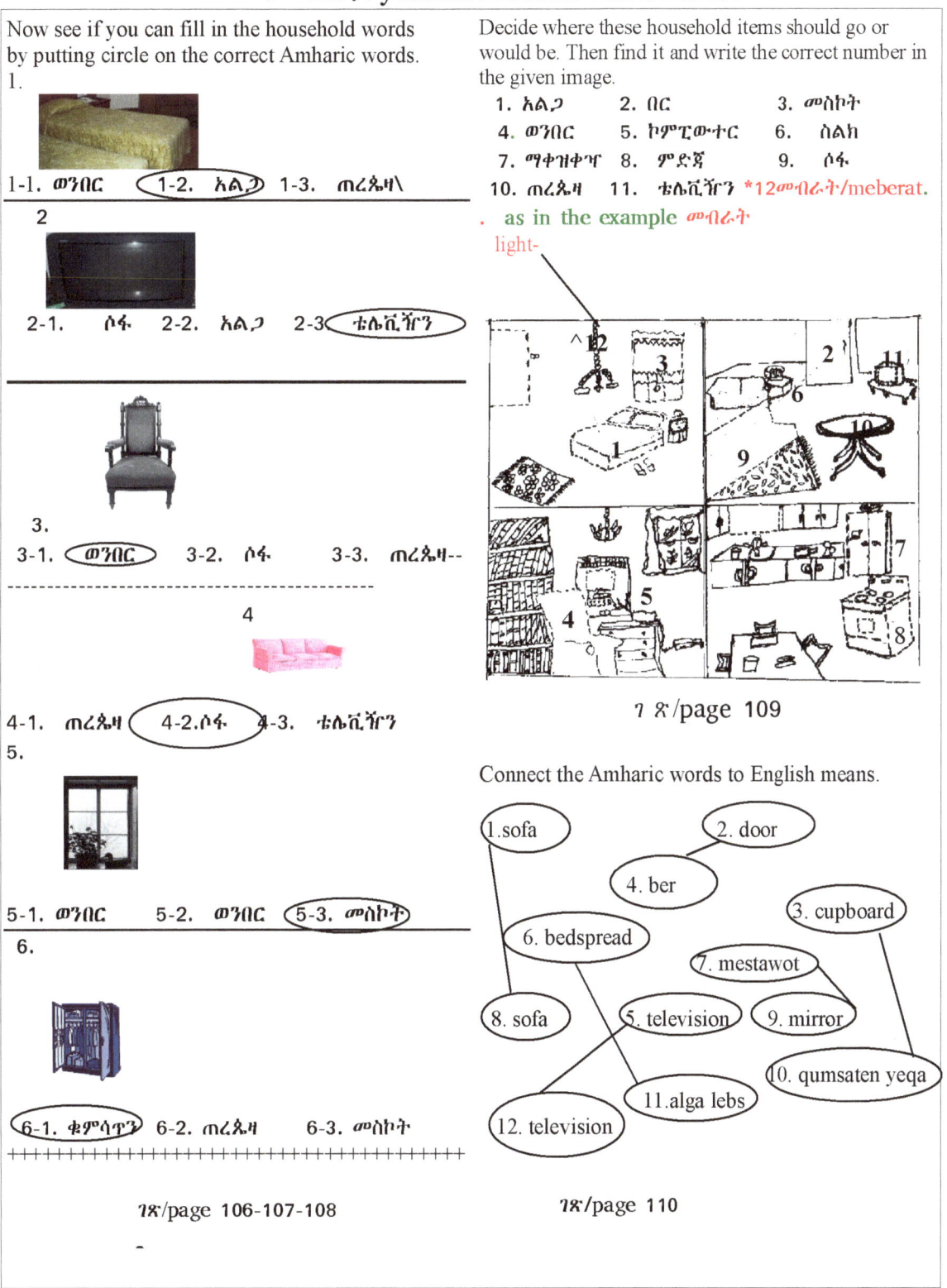

Now see if you can fill in the household words by putting circle on the correct Amharic words.

1.
1-1. ወንበር   1-2. (አልጋ)   1-3. ጠረጴዛ\

2.
2-1. ሶፋ   2-2. አልጋ   2-3. (ቴሌቪዥን)

3.
3-1. (ወንበር)   3-2. ሶፋ   3-3. ጠረጴዛ

4.
4-1. ጠረጴዛ   (4-2. ሶፋ)   4-3. ቴሌቪዥን

5.
5-1. ወንበር   5-2. ወንበር   (5-3. መስኮት)

6.
(6-1. ቁምሳጥን)   6-2. ጠረጴዛ   6-3. መስኮት

+++

ገጽ/page 106-107-108

Decide where these household items should go or would be. Then find it and write the correct number in the given image.

1. አልጋ   2. በር   3. መስኮት
4. ወንበር   5. ኮምፒውተር   6. ስልክ
7. ማቀዝቀዣ   8. ምድጃ   9. ሶፋ
10. ጠረጴዛ   11. ቴሌቪዥን   *12መብራት/meberat.

as in the example መብራት light-

ገጽ/page 109

Connect the Amharic words to English means.

1. sofa
2. door
3. cupboard
4. ber
5. television
6. bedspread
7. mestawot
8. sofa
9. mirror
10. qumsaten yeqa
11. alga lebs
12. television

ገጽ/page 110

ማመሳከሪያ/yemamesakeria-corroborate

Decide where the house hold items should go. Then write the correct numbers by the picture, as in the example.

ምሳሌ/mesaley-example *6 ስልክ -i

1 አልጋ-g 2 በር-a 3. መስኮት-k 4. ወንበር-b 5. ኮፒውተር-j 6* ስልክ-i   7 ማቀዝቀዣ -e
8 ምድጃ-f 9 ሶፋ-l 10. ጠረጴዛ-c 11 ቴለቪዥን-d   12 ሰዓት-h

a. 2
b. 4
c. 10
d. 11
7-e
8-f
1-g
h. 12
i. example 6
j-5
k 3
l. 9

ገጽ/page 111

ገጽ/page 181

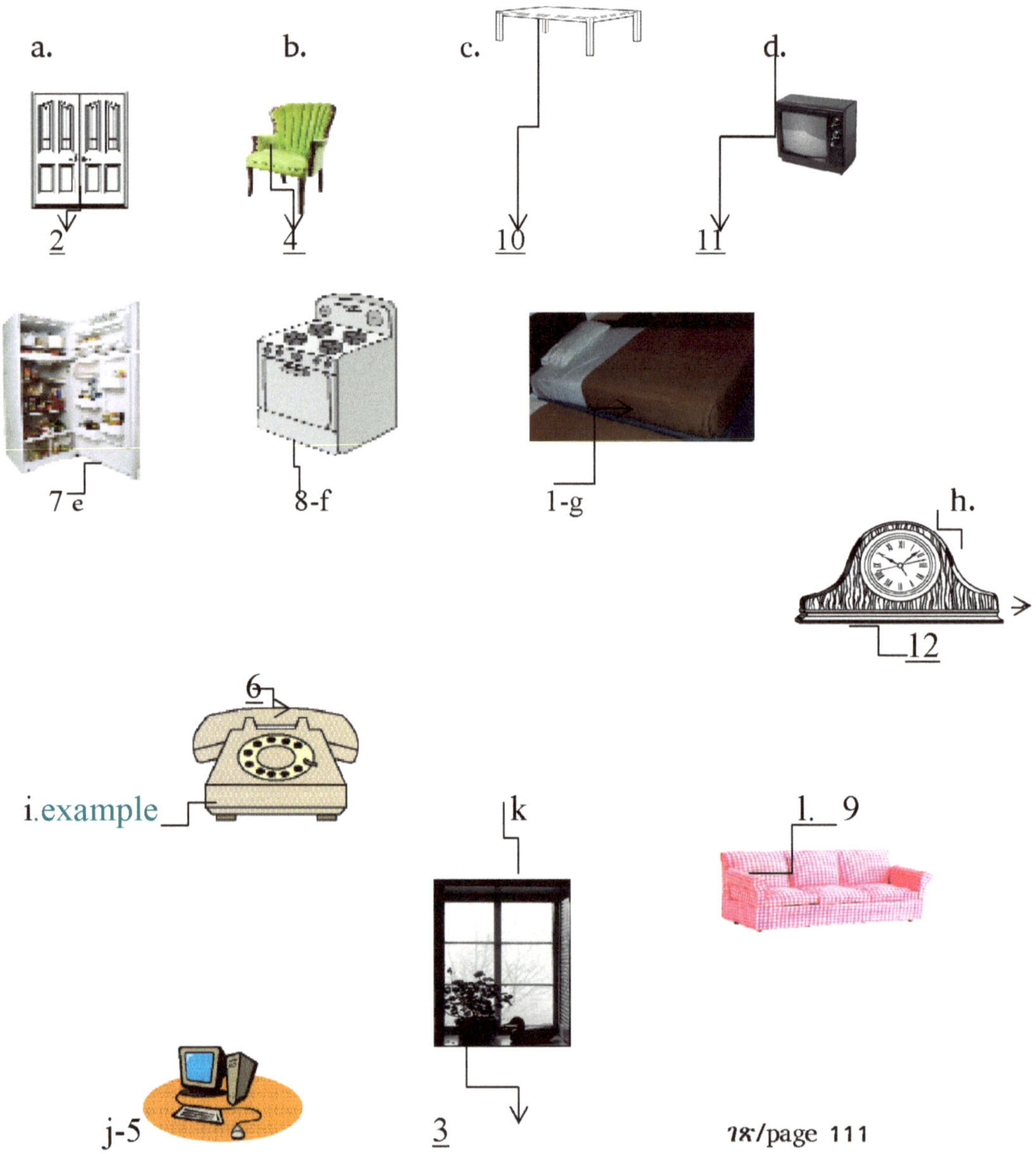

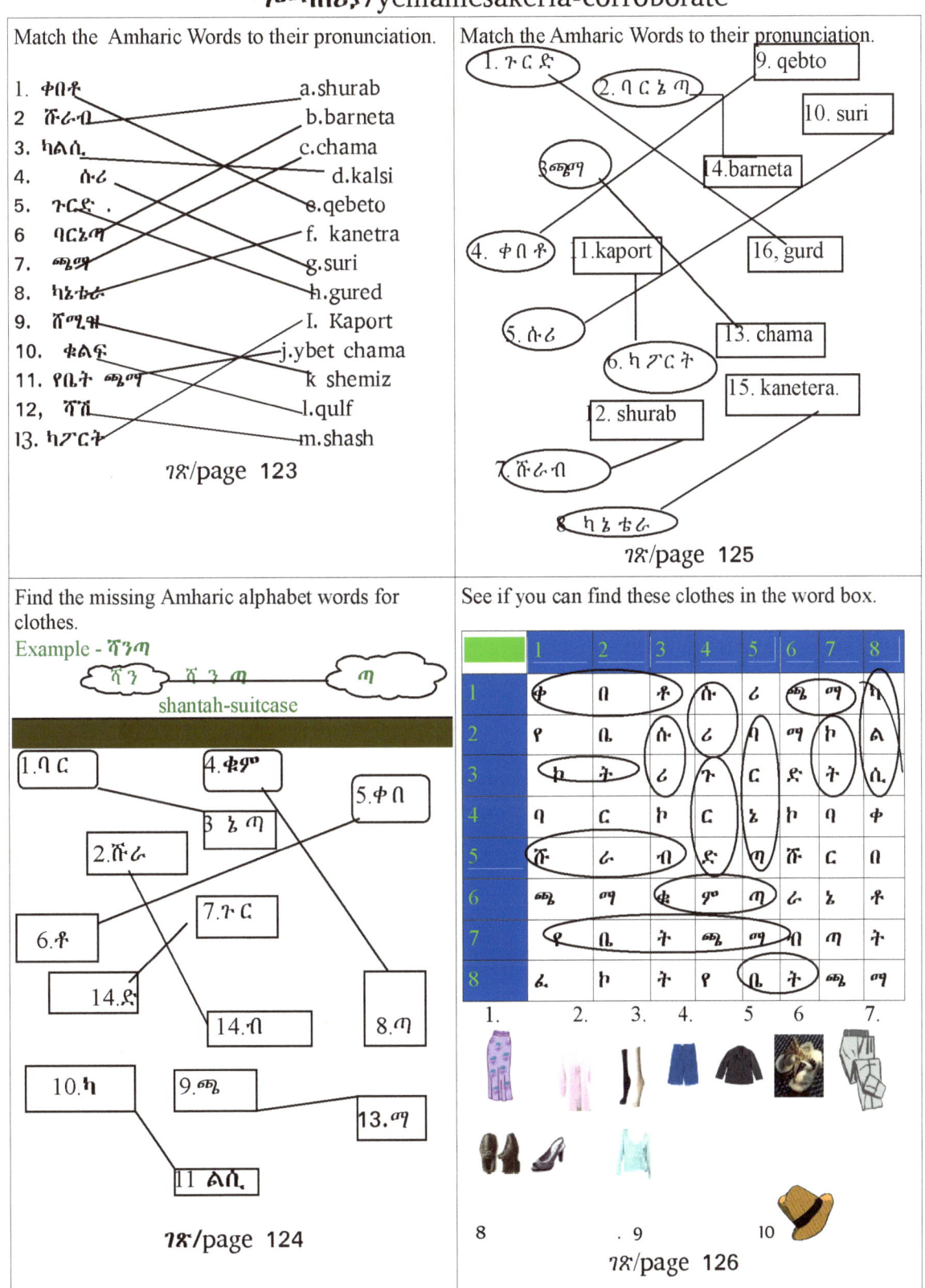

ማመሳከሪያ/yemamesakeria-corroborate

Babule is going on vacation, count how many of ach type of clothing she is packing in her suitcase,

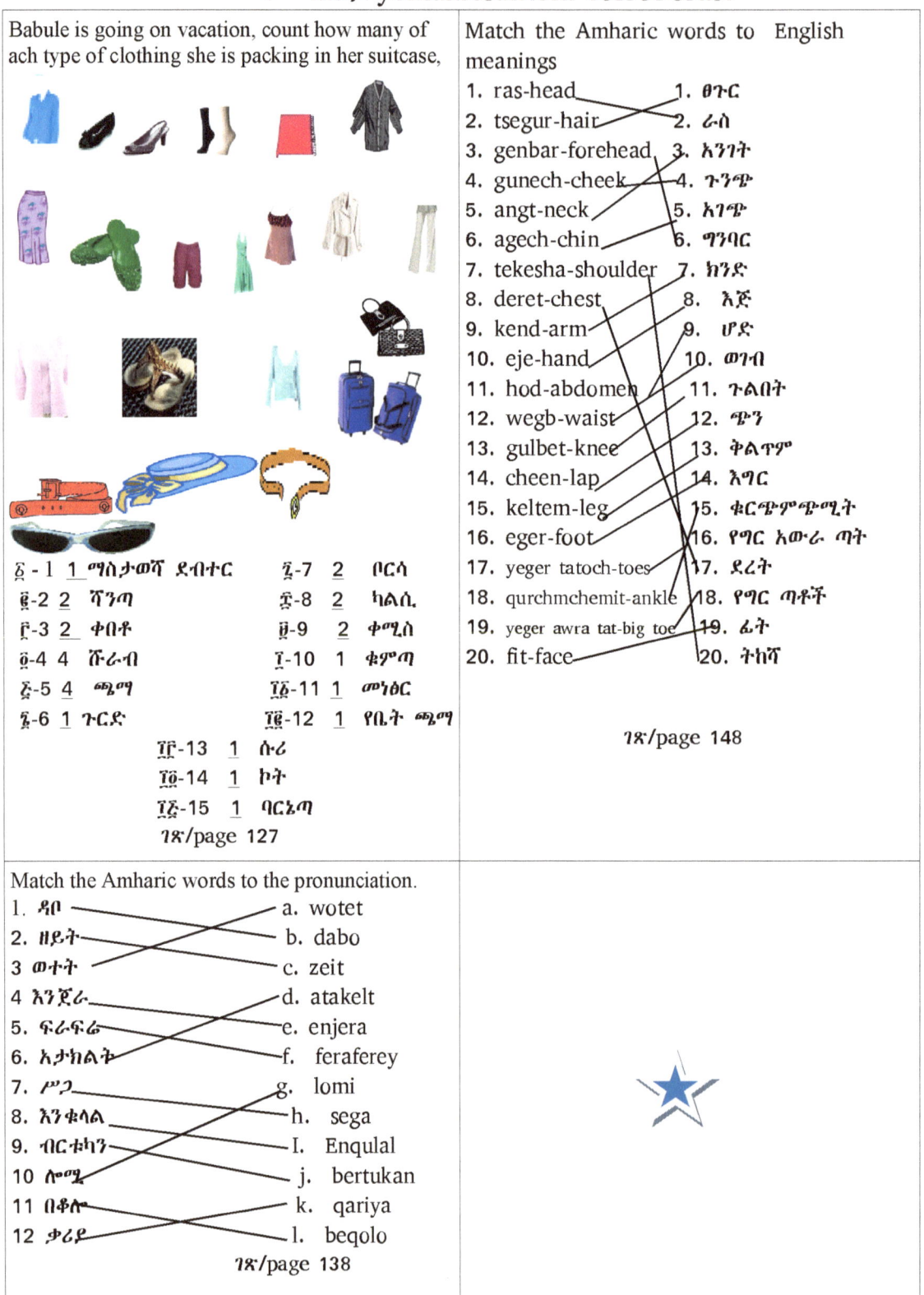

፩-1	1	ማስታወሻ ደብተር	፯-7	2	ቦርሳ
፪-2	2	ሻንጣ	፰-8	2	ካልሲ
፫-3	2	ቀበቶ	፱-9	2	ቀሚስ
፬-4	4	ሹራብ	፲-10	1	ቁምጣ
፭-5	4	ጫማ	፲፩-11	1	መነፅር
፮-6	1	ጉርድ	፲፪-12	1	የቤት ጫማ
			፲፫-13	1	ሱሪ
			፲፬-14	1	ኮት
			፲፭-15	1	ባርኔጣ

ገጽ/page 127

Match the Amharic words to English meanings

1. ras-head — 1. ፀጉር
2. tsegur-hair — 2. ራስ
3. genbar-forehead — 3. አንገት
4. gunech-cheek — 4. ጉንጭ
5. angt-neck — 5. አገጭ
6. agech-chin — 6. ግንባር
7. tekesha-shoulder — 7. ክንድ
8. deret-chest — 8. እጅ
9. kend-arm — 9. ሆድ
10. eje-hand — 10. ወገብ
11. hod-abdomen — 11. ጉልበት
12. wegb-waist — 12. ጭን
13. gulbet-knee — 13. ቅልጥም
14. cheen-lap — 14. እግር
15. keltem-leg — 15. ቁርጭምጭሚት
16. eger-foot — 16. የግር አውራ ጣት
17. yeger tatoch-toes — 17. ደረት
18. qurchmchemit-ankle — 18. የግር ጣቶች
19. yeger awra tat-big toe — 19. ፊት
20. fit-face — 20. ትከሻ

ገጽ/page 148

Match the Amharic words to the pronunciation.

1. ዳቦ — a. wotet
2. ዘይት — b. dabo
3. ወተት — c. zeit
4. እንጀራ — d. atakelt
5. ፍራፍሬ — e. enjera
6. አታክልት — f. feraferey
7. ሎጋ — g. lomi
8. እንቁላል — h. sega
9. ብርቱካን — I. Enqulal
10. ሎሚ — j. bertukan
11. በቆሎ — k. qariya
12. ቃሪያ — l. beqolo

ገጽ/page 138

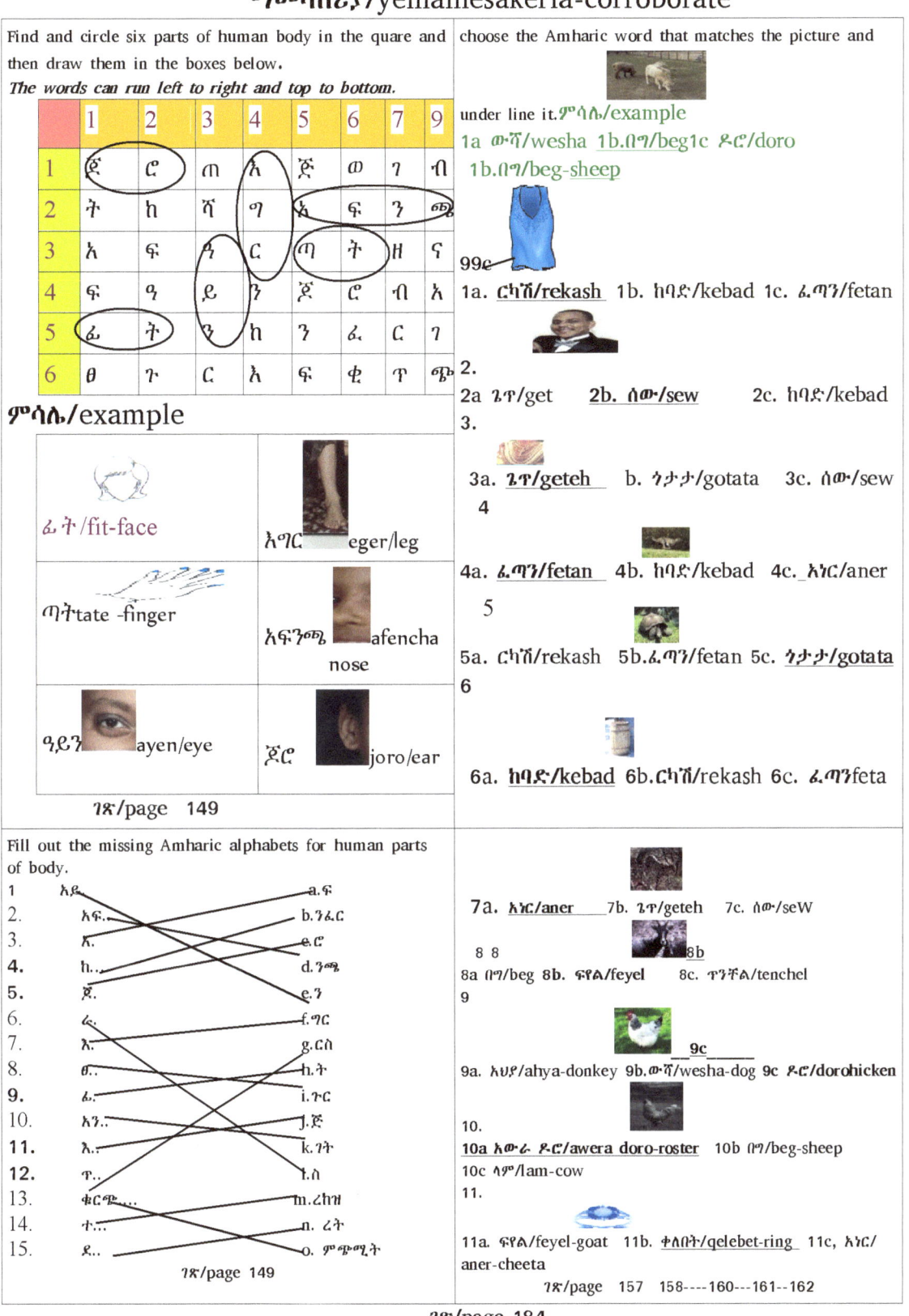

ማመሳከሪያ/yemamesakeria-corroborate

Find the Amharic words and connect it to their pronunciation.

- a ሰኞ
- 6 qedamey
- 1 segno
- b ማክሰኞ
- 4 hamus
- 7 ehud
- f ቅዳሜ
- c ረቡዕ
- 3 rebue
- 2 maxsegno
- g እሁድ
- 5 arbe
- d ሐሙስ
- e ዓርብ

ገጽ/page 164

Look at these Amharic words pronunciations and Identify it which word is belong to months then write in Amharic on given spaces if not put X.

1. teqemet huletegnaw wor now. ጥቅምት
   ጥቅምት ሁለተኛው ወር ነው።
2. seney zenab ynoral. ሰኔ
   ሰኔ ዝናብ ይኖራል።
3. qedamey ena ehud yereft gize now. X
   ቅዳሜ እና እሁድ የረፍት ጊዜ ነው።
4. pagumey yeametu mecheresha wor now. ጳጉሜ
   ጳጉሜ ያመቱ መጨርረሻ ወር ነው።
5. sostengaw wor man yebalale? ህዳር
6. hulet weroch sem tsaf ነሃሴ ህዳር
   ሁለት ወሮች ስም ጻፍ።
7. ter sentegnaw wer now? አምስተኛው
   ጥር ሰንተኛው ወር ነው።
8. ledeteh/tesh yetegnaw wer lay now? ግንቦት
   ልደትህ/ሽ የትኛው ወር ላይ ነው።
9. hameley,nehasey yezeb werat now ሐምሌ፤ ነሃሴ
   ሐምሌ፤ ነሃሴ የዘናብ ወራት ነው።
10. ye ehetey ledet be miyazya woost now ሚያዝያ
    የ እህቴ ልደት በሚያዝያ ውስጥ ነው።

ገጽ/page 167

Match the Amharic words to their pronunciation.

1. meskerem-September — a መጋቢት
2. hedar-November — b ጥቅምት
3. yekatit-February — c የካቲት
4. megabit-March — d ግንቦት
5. miyaziya- April — e ህዳር
6. teqmet-October — f ሰኔ
7. tahesas-December — g መስከረም
8. genbot-may — h ሚያዝያ
9. hamley-July — I ነሃሴ-
10. seney-June — j ጥር
11. nehasey-August — k ጳጉሜ
12. ter-January — l ሐምሌ
13. pagumey-pagumey — m ታህሳስ

ገጽ/page 166

Match the Amharic word to English meaning.

1. ሰማያዊ/blue — a. hamerawi
2. ጥቁር/black — b. bicha
3. ቀይ/red — c. weha semayawi
4. ሃምራዊ/rose — d. qey
5. ቢጫ/yello — e. bunama
6. አረንጓዴ/green — f. semayawi
7. ውሃ ሰማያዊ/light blue — g. tequr
8. ወይን ጠጅ/purple — h. arenguwadey
9. ቡናማ/brown — I. gracha
10. ብርማ/siliver — J. tequr qey
11. ነጭ/white — k. weteney
12. ብርቱካን/Orange — l. berma
13. ውጢኔ/bright orange — m weyn tej
14. ጥቁር ቀይ/dark red — n nech
15. ግራጫ/gray — o bertukan

ገጽ/page 171

ገጽ/page 185

ማመሳከሪያ/yemamesakeria-corroborate

Find the Ethiopian and American Flag-color words in the box below. See how many new words you can find and log them.

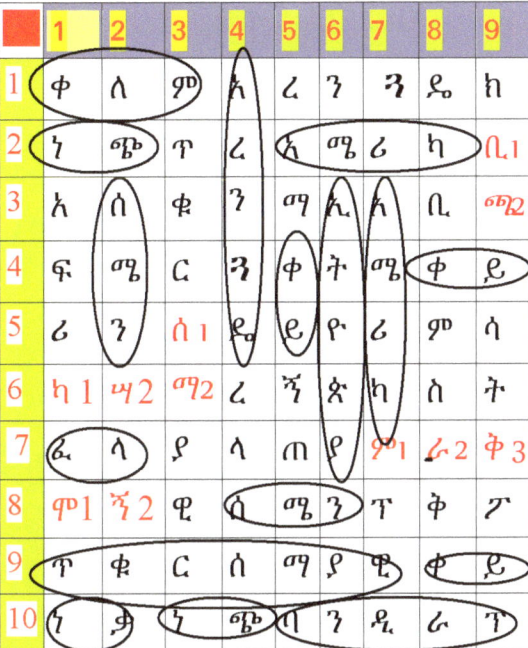

1 ቢጫ
2 ሰማ
3 ካሣ
4 ምራቅ
5 ሞኝ

ገጽ/page 173

Who is ESAC??

ESAC is a nonprofit public benefit organization and is established for the community's services of any race without difference. It is organized under the nonprofit public Benefit Corporation Law for welfare and education purposes.

Mission

1. To empower the local Ethiopian community and community at large enhance the educational. Economical, cultural and social well being of community thereby improving the life of the community

2. In addition culture, women rights and health initiatives will be implemented programs to increase the educational standards and identify new goals. Health programs to coordinate initiatives in every aspect of the healthcare delivery system, as well as securing domestic and international volunteers.

3. To advocate issues important to women's right, lanuage, culture and history influence local policy, encourage networking and assist needy to adapt the American system of life.

The primary objectives

The organization includes providing material, language, culture, educational programs, social assistance and counseling services to immigrant families, elders, children and youth in order to help them integrate within a new cultural and socio-economical system of the United States.

www.ingramcontent.com/pod-product-compliance
Lightning Source LLC
Chambersburg PA
CBHW041540220426
43664CB00002B/13